The life of Verdi

Musical lives

Each book in this series describes the life and music of a major composer, revealing the private as well as the public figure. While the main thread is biographical, the music appears as an integral part of the narrative, each volume thus presenting an organic view of the composer, the music and the circumstances in which the music was written.

Published titles

The life of Beethoven DAVID WYN JONES
The life of Bellini JOHN ROSSELLI
The life of Berlioz PETER BLOOM
The life of Debussy ROGER NICHOLS
The life of Charles Ives STUART FEDER
The life of Mahler PETER FRANKLIN
The life of Mendelssohn PETER MERCER-TAYLOR
The life of Mozart JOHN ROSSELLI
The life of Musorgsky CARYL EMERSON
The life of Schubert CHRISTOPHER H. GIBBS
The life of Richard Strauss BRYAN GILLIAM
The life of Verdi JOHN ROSSELLI
The life of Webern KATHRYN BAILEY

The life of Verdi

JOHN ROSSELLI

CAMBRIDGE
UNIVERSITY PRESS

PUBLISHED BY THE PRESS SYNDICATE OF THE UNIVERSITY OF CAMBRIDGE
The Pitt Building, Trumpington Street, Cambridge, United Kingdom

CAMBRIDGE UNIVERSITY PRESS
The Edinburgh Building, Cambridge CB2 2RU, UK
40 West 20th Street, New York, NY 10011–4211, USA
477 Williamstown Road, Port Melbourne, VIC 3207, Australia
Ruiz de Alarcón 13, 28014 Madrid, Spain
Dock House, The Waterfront, Cape Town 8001, South Africa

http://www.cambridge.org

© Cambridge University Press 2000

This book is in copyright. Subject to statutory exception
and to the provisions of relevant collective licensing agreements,
no reproduction of any part may take place without
the written permission of Cambridge University Press.

First published 2000
Reprinted 2001 (twice)

Printed in the United Kingdom at the University Press, Cambridge

Typeface FF Quadraat 9.75/14 pt   *System* QuarkXPress™ [SE]

A catalogue record for this book is available from the British Library

Library of Congress cataloguing in publication data

Rosselli, John.
The life of Verdi / John Rosselli.
  p. cm.   (Musical lives)
Includes bibliographical references and index.
ISBN 0 521 66011 4 – ISBN 0 521 66957 X (pbk.)
1. Verdi, Giusepe, 1813–1901. 2. Composers – Italy – Biography. I. Title. II. Series.
ML410.V4   R74   2000
782.1′092–dc21
[B]   99-059952

ISBN 0 521 66011 4   hardback
ISBN 0 521 66957 X   paperback

CONTENTS

List of illustrations vi
Preface ix
List of abbreviations used in source references xi
Introduction: truth and theatre 1

1 The innkeeper's son, 1813–1842: *Oberto* to *Nabucco* 9
2 The galley slave, 1842–1847: *Nabucco* to *Macbeth* 34
3 Turning-points, 1847–1849: *I masnadieri* to *La battaglia di Legnano*; Strepponi, revolution and Sant'Agata 61
4 The people's composer, 1849–1859: *Luisa Miller* to *Un ballo in maschera* 86
5 Complications, 1859–1872: *La forza del destino*, *Don Carlos*, and *Aida* 121
6 Evergreen, 1872–1901: the Requiem, *Otello*, and *Falstaff* 155

Notes 188
Further reading 197
Index 200

ILLUSTRATIONS

(Unless otherwise stated, provenance is the Istituto Nazionale di Studi Verdiani, Parma)
1 The so-called birthplace at Roncole, near Busseto, in fact the inn where the boy Verdi grew up, from an old postcard *page* 13
2 Antonio Barezzi, Verdi's 'second father' and father-in-law 16
3 Margherita Barezzi, Verdi's first wife. Oil painting by Augusto Mussini, Museo Teatrale alla Scala, Milan 26
4 Verdi about the time of his breakthrough with *Nabucco*, 1842. Anonymous lithograph 32
5 Caricature statuette of Verdi by Dantan Jeune, 1866. The original is at Sant'Agata 40
6 Verdi's chief librettist Francesco Maria Piave, with whom he collaborated from 1843 to 1862. Portrait by G. Favretto 46
7 The smoking ruins of Aquileia: sketch for the first scene of *Attila* (Venice, La Fenice, 1846) by the stage designer Giuseppe Bertoja 55
8 Verdi in his late thirties 60
9 Giuseppina Strepponi as Nina in Pietro Coppola's opera, which she sang in Venice in 1835–36 at the age of twenty. Contemporary engraving 67
10 Two views of *Rigoletto*, Act 3
    (a) In the imaginary setting used as frontispiece of the original vocal score, Sparafucile's tavern is a modest building (Raccolta delle Stampe Bertarelli, Milan); (b) Giuseppe Bertoja's original stage design: the prestige of the Teatro La Fenice demanded that the tavern should look implausibly grand 96–7
11 Giuseppe Bertoja's design for Act 1, scene 2 of *Il trovatore* at La Fenice, Venice 104
12 Verdi rehearsing *Simon Boccanegra* in Naples, 1858, with the poodle Loulou in attendance. Caricature by Melchiorre Delfico 115
13 Verdi at the time of *Il Trovatore*, probably of the French version (1857) since he is wearing the French Legion of Honour 120

Illustrations vii

14 Verdi's house at Sant'Agata at an early stage of development. The original house has been added to but the trees have not yet grown to full height. Contemporary engraving 129
15 The conductor Angelo Mariani 137
16 Verdi's disciple and only student Emanuele Muzio 138
17 Verdi at the time of *Aida*, 1872. Bust by Vincenzo Gemito. Several versions exist; this one is at Sant'Agata 142
18 Giuseppina Strepponi in her sixties 144
19 Why Verdi admired the production values at the Paris Opéra: *Aida*, Act 3, 1880. Contemporary engraving, Raccolta delle Stampe Bertarelli, Milan 153
20 Giulio Ricordi, shown as the quintessence of fin-de-siècle aestheticising Italian culture, a strong contrast to Verdi's earlier, earthier Italy. Copyright © Casa Ricordi, Milan 157
21 Verdi in his seventies 162
22 Verdi's study in Sant'Agata 168
23 Otello overhears Cassio and Iago joking about the handkerchief in the original Milan production, 1887. Contemporary engraving, Raccolta delle Stampe Bertarelli, Milan 174
24 Verdi in the garden at Sant'Agata in extreme old age, with his sister-in-law Barberina Strepponi (seated, second from left), Teresa Stolz (standing, left), and Giulio Ricordi (standing, second from right) among others 185
    Map Italy in 1815, after the restoration of the old sovereigns overthrown by Napoleon 11

PREFACE

This is a short critical life based on the very full published sources. It sets out not to provide new facts but to show Verdi in his historical context and thereby throw light – at times new – on the significance of his life and work. Lives of Verdi are many; some are highly detailed. A short book necessarily picks out certain episodes and works as more important than others. Where critics have written unimprovably on the music I have at times quoted them.

Verdi and his Italian contemporaries often used three full stops as a rhetorical device; these are reproduced in quotations. To show breaks in quotations I have used full stops within square brackets: [. . .]. Verdi and others also frequently used '!!!', '!?', '!!?' and so on; these too are reproduced. Such lavish punctuation does not convey the extremes of surprise, horror etc. it would suggest in an English-speaking writer; it probably sets out to render what gesture would do in conversation.

As the section on further reading explains more fully, there is as yet no complete edition of Verdi's letters in Italian, and only a limited choice in English; letters appear in many places. When I have quoted from the richest sources of Verdi's own words and those of his second wife Giuseppina Strepponi, I have appended in brackets an abbreviation identifying the source, followed by the page number(s); sources of other quotations appear in an end note. Where a source exists in an easily available English translation, references are as a rule given to that; this is particularly true of Frank Walker's translations of Strepponi's letters, some of which appeared in print before the originals. I have, however, often made my own translation from Verdi's letters. A list of abbreviations follows.

I am most grateful for help in finding illustrative material to Marisa

Di Gregorio Casati of the Istituto Nazionale di Studi Verdiani at Parma, for help and friendship over a long period to the director of the Institute, Pierluigi Petrobelli, and to Alberto Carrara-Verdi and his family for their kindness in showing me over Sant'Agata.

J. R.

ABBREVIATIONS USED IN SOURCE REFERENCES

A F. Abbiati, *Giuseppe Verdi*, 4 vols., Milan, 1959

BM M. Conati, *La bottega della musica. Verdi e la Fenice*, Milan, 1983

C *I copialettere di Giuseppe Verdi*, ed. G. Cesari and A. Luzio, Milan, 1913, facsimile reprint Sala Bolognese, 1987

CV *Carteggi verdiani*, ed. A. Luzio, 4 vols., Rome, 1935, 1947

IEV *Interviews and encounters with Verdi*, ed. M. Conati, London, 1984

VB *Carteggio Verdi-Boito*, ed. M. Medici, M. Conati, and M. Casati, 2 vols. [pagination continuous], Parma, 1978

VI *Verdi intimo. Carteggio di Giuseppe Verdi con il conte Opprandino Arrivabene (1861–1886)*, ed. A. Alberti, Milan, 1931

VR 80–81 *Carteggio Verdi-Ricordi 1880–1881*, ed. P. Petrobelli, M. Di Gregorio Casati, and C. M. Mossa, Parma, 1988

VR 82–85 *Carteggio Verdi-Ricordi 1882–1885*, ed. F. Cella, M. Ricordi, and M. Di Gregorio Casati, Parma, 1994

WalkerV F. Walker, *The Man Verdi*, London, 1962

Introduction: truth and theatre

Among composers of genius – the philosopher Isaiah Berlin wrote in a famous essay – Verdi was 'perhaps the last complete, self-fulfilled creator [. . .] a man who dissolved everything in his art'. That art, like Bach's, like Shakespeare's, was 'objective, direct, and in harmony with the conventions which govern it'; it sprang 'from an unbroken inner unity, a sense of belonging to its own time and society and milieu'; it had nothing to do with the reaching out after something lost, infinite, unattainable that marked more self-conscious artists like Berlioz or Wagner. All this made Verdi 'the last great voice of humanism not at war with itself, at any rate in music [. . .] the last master to paint with positive, clear, primary colours, to give direct expression to the eternal, major human emotions [. . .]. Noble, simple, with a degree of unbroken vitality and vast natural power of creation', Verdi's voice – perhaps just because it came from 'a world which is no more' – spoke urgently both to sophisticated and to ordinary hearers in our own time.[1]

Berlin's analysis – in some ways questionable – brings out what many have felt when confronted with Verdi's works. Whatever their defects, those works ring emotionally true; truth and directness make them exciting, often hugely so. Yet they nearly all belong to the most artificial of genres – not just opera but Italian romantic opera, written to agreed formulas for enactment by singers of outstanding gifts, set within a proscenium arch amid illusionistic scenery, before an audience visibly arrayed in tiers of boxes. Verdi's twenty-six operas (twenty-eight, if we count major revisions) are at once truth and theatre.

Verdi himself knew that his vocation to write for the theatre meant pleasing the public and filling the house. 'The box office', he wrote late in his career, 'is the proper thermometer of success.'[2] Even in his venerated old age, empty seats at the first performance of his Sacred Pieces meant failure. At most, if he was convinced that a seeming failure was worth while, as with *La traviata* in 1853, he shrugged, said 'time will tell', and took care to revise the work so that it triumphed next time round (BM, 326–7). Never, it seemed, would he let himself be taken for a misunderstood genius.

Today he could rest content: he is one of only four composers (the others are Mozart, Wagner, and Puccini) whose works nearly always fill an opera house. Verdi's achieved this even between 1890 and 1930, when the composer's reputation was in eclipse among the musically educated. True, the popular works (*Rigoletto*, *Trovatore*, *Traviata*, and *Aida*) filled theatres equally popular in their social make-up, while élite houses might at times neglect them or fling them on to the stage as box-office fodder. The cognoscenti tended to approve only the refined products of the composer's old age, *Otello* and *Falstaff*; the early operas and the more problematic later works were almost nowhere. People who first came to music in the 1930s recall how some of the knowledgeable shuddered at anything so 'vulgar' as 'La donna è mobile' or the triumphal march from *Aida*.

Today all is changed. Even an opera Verdi himself set aside and cannibalised, *Stiffelio*, has been pieced together, performed with great success, and recorded. The most blatant of his early works, *Attila*, still raised a few titters at Sadler's Wells in 1963; by 1990 at Covent Garden it won roars of approval.

In its dip and rise the curve of Verdi's reputation matches that of some great novelists who were his close contemporaries, Dickens in particular. Mocked in his own time as 'Mr Popular Sentiment' – just as

Verdi was called crude, noisy, and melodramatic – Dickens, about 1900, seemed a writer to be indulged for his comic turns; only in the past fifty years or so have *Bleak House*, *Little Dorrit*, and *Our Mutual Friend* been studied as great works of art, intricately wrought out of a wide and deep vision of society. Not by accident, that period has also brought a mighty growth of serious critical interest in Verdi: he now earns the attention once confined to Beethoven or Wagner.

For nineteenth-century Italians, opera did what the Italian novel failed to do (Manzoni's *The Betrothed* apart): it both crystallised feelings and relationships in which they could see themselves and let them attain new heights of imaginative experience, grounded in thrilling melodramatic action. Verdi's operas were the Italian equivalent not just of Dickens's but of Victor Hugo's or Dostoevsky's novels, where likewise action at times violent or lurid served to deepen insight into human life. Thanks to the power of music and to Verdi's individual strengths the operas now work in the theatre through almost the whole of their course as, in the reader's perception, the novels do not. Hugo's swollen rhetoric, Dostoevsky's rant, Dickens's false sentiment over young women alienate us from parts of their works; Verdi's early operas are at times blatant or ramshackle, but – as with the Covent Garden *Attila* – a good performance in the theatre lets their joined energy and nobility carry all before them.

Our perceptions have in some ways caught up with Verdi's methods. Critics as late as the 1950s tended to smile at his lightning changes of mood: a character rushes on (Amonasro in the Nile scene in *Aida*, say) and the situation changes catastrophically within two or three bars. No one these days seems to notice – probably because we have got used to the jump-cut technique of films made since the New Wave broke in 1959, which has spread to the theatre and to television drama, not to mention advertising videos. In anticipating the jump-cut Verdi was not so much prophetic as impatient: to make his operas work in the theatre he again and again demanded fewer words, more rapid action; he praised the 'supreme courage' that cut good things for the sake of speed (C, 631); he echoed the saying attributed to

Voltaire, 'I allow all genres except the boring genre.' Verdi's operas are not boring.

If, as Berlin maintained, Verdi 'is his work, for his work is himself', one might expect the composer's life to show the kind of blazing, immediate truth conveyed by the operas. Yet as scholars bring out new details of his career Verdi is often found speaking less than the literal truth. Biographers must decide what to make of this.

He was not even born in the house that came to be revered in his lifetime as his birthplace, or in the year he – as he claimed – for most of his life thought he had been born in. Yet he must have known about his true place of birth (his parents went on living in it till he was thirteen); moving as he did among petty despotic states that required him at every step to show his birth certificate or passport, can he have failed to notice the year correctly named in those documents? The most notorious such slip is Verdi's account of the deaths of his first wife and their two children: he told two biographers, in 1869 and again in 1881, that all three had died in 1840 within three months. In fact the children had died in 1838 and 1839 and his wife in 1840; this harrowing march of death had taken nearly two years.

Another kind of doubt springs from Verdi's account of the libretto for his Paris opera *Les Vêpres siciliennes* (1855). The librettist, Eugène Scribe, had originally written it for an abortive opera by Donizetti; the subject at that time was the Duke of Alva, the scourge of the sixteenth-century Netherlands. Well after Donizetti's death, Scribe re-used and adapted it for Verdi; it now dealt with the Sicilian revolt against an older tyrannical rule. When, in 1882, Donizetti's *Le Duc d'Albe* was at length performed (in an Italian version completed by another hand), Verdi stated that he had known nothing of it; yet his correspondence in the run-up to the 1855 opera shows that he had.

Again, in a dispute with his publisher Ricordi over the French rights to his opera *Luisa Miller*, Verdi accused Ricordi of having bamboozled him by getting him to sign a contract without pointing out a damaging clause, so that he had failed to notice it. The rest of Verdi's business correspondence shows him unfailingly alert to the terms of contracts; it seems most likely that he made his charge because, for reasons to be dealt with later, he was angry at having had to give up all the rights in *Luisa* for a fee much lower than he had got used to, and was doing all he could to recoup himself. (The fuss he made worked: Ricordi cut him in on the French rights.)

Last, while Verdi in old age was writing *Falstaff* – keeping it private, with many reservations in what he told the few people in the know: it was a pastime, he might not finish it – he stated publicly in April 1890 that *Otello*, performed three years earlier, was his last work: 'the decision is irrevocable [. . .] my task is finished'. Yet on 17 March he had finished Act I of *Falstaff*.[3]

For these slips, and a number of others, there may be varying explanations. In Mediterranean societies a sense of drama easily shapes a conversation; those taking part may say outrageous things which, if challenged, they would qualify. Verdi's account of the deaths of his wife and children may fall under this head: it *felt* like a hell of pain unrolling through continuous weeks. Wanting to get his own way and to give the impression he chose may explain some of the misstatements about professional and business matters; if so Verdi behaved like many present-day businessmen, not only Mediterranean ones.

He was indeed the most businesslike of composers. His businesslike conduct at most times alerts us to the disconcerting moments when he told less than the truth. Such moments are far outnumbered by the many instances of Verdi's plain dealing and his determination to meet his commitments (and to see that others met theirs). But his very diligence in keeping up and filing away his correspondence, at a time when letters were quickly and reliably delivered and easily kept, tended to preserve every kind of evidence, including some that showed him as inconsistent or not quite truthful.

Like his contemporary Gladstone, Verdi lived through nine-tenths of a century when people of means communicated by letters written for the most part on long-lasting paper. Each of the two men carried on a steady correspondence with many people, often keeping copies or minutes of his own side; each was famous from an early age, so that his acquaintances tended to keep his letters; each lived to see the telephone but scarcely to use it; each acquired a large house, undisturbed at his death (Verdi's still belongs to his heirs), where the evidence of his manifold activity could be stored. The result in each case is vast archives such as we shall never see the like of in the age of e-mail and fax; happily for his biographers, Verdi was laconic where Gladstone was prolix.

Another notable difference is that where Gladstone's diary has, in our own time, given away some of his convoluted inner life, Verdi defended the privacy of his personal ties and emotions, fiercely and with remarkable success. Though we know a great deal about his professional career, we still know almost nothing about his brief first marriage, and little more about some crucial episodes in his relationship (through nearly sixty years) with his second wife; the crisis in his second marriage over the singer Teresa Stolz, friend to both husband and wife, has come under intense scrutiny but remains in part baffling. More generally, Verdi's sexual life is a closed book. We are left – a good thing perhaps – to plumb, from the evidence of his life and work, the deeper truthfulness that ruled both.

Here we move beyond the kind of truth that concerns a judge and jury. 'A refining of the sense of truthfulness' – Willa Cather wrote in her novel about a great opera singer, *The Song of the Lark* – is the mark of artistic growth: 'The stupid believe that to be truthful is easy; only the artist, the great artist, knows how difficult it is.' Verdi himself said as much. At a time (1876) when *verismo* was in the air – the Italian term for naturalism – he wrote: 'copying the truth may be a good thing, but *inventing the truth* is better, much better'; the difference was that between photography and painting (C, 624).

So far, both Cather and Verdi have in mind the truth in what an artist makes or enacts. We say that it 'rings' true, 'convinces', 'hits us in the solar plexus' – all attempts at putting into words our sense of a communication we can take in unalloyed and wholeheartedly make our own.

Whether our assent says anything about the artist's personal truthfulness is a moot point. Many artists put the best of themselves into their work; to go from that to their everyday lives and opinions may disconcert. Wagner is a well-known example. As for Verdi, those writers who, since Carlo Gatti's 1931 biography, have pointed out his exaggerations and misstatements have all shown that they none the less admired him as a man, faults and all.

A personal statement. Working on this book has led me to conclude that I do not very much like the man Verdi, in particular the autocratic rentier-cum-estate owner, part-time composer, and seemingly full-time grumbler and reactionary critic of the later years, from about 1860; yet it has deepened my admiration and respect for him, indeed my trust. Verdi can be trusted in a fundamental sense: not only would one rather have professional or business dealings with him – at the cost of some rough moments – than with many other people; a deep integrity runs beneath his life, and can be felt even when he is being unreasonable or wrong. This guiding thread helps to explain the astonishing self-renewal that marked Verdi's life – one that spanned the Napoleonic empire and the age of broadcasting. The biographer's task is to hold on to this guiding thread without blinking the awkward moments, but also without niggling over them.

A biographer writing in this series must also make hard choices. Verdi's legacy is at once the supreme product of Italian opera and a highly individual body of work, shaped by an original mind that went its own way: a live refutation of the theory that 'writing' is all, one text is as good as another, and individual creativity does not matter. There is a lot of it and we know a great deal about the making of it. The music must be considered – it is after all the reason why Verdi interests us – but, in this format, only some of the operas and the Requiem. I assume that the truly important works are the indestructible quartet already named (*Rigoletto, Trovatore, Traviata, Aida*), followed at a slight distance by *Un ballo in maschera* and, among the early works, by *Ernani* and *Macbeth*, among the late ones, by *Don Carlos, Otello*, and *Falstaff*. This means saying little about fine works such as *Luisa Miller*, *Simon Boccanegra*, and *La forza del destino*, and, at times, less than one would like about the chosen operas themselves.

That long life too must be taken as something other than a continuous chain of events. Verdi's professional career falls into distinct phases. He was first – down to the 1848–49 revolutions and *La battaglia di Legnano* – the 'galley slave' who won ready success at the cost of writing on average two operas a year; then, through the 1850s – from *Rigoletto* to *Un ballo in maschera* – the master whose works achieved unprecedented, literally world-wide popularity. The wealth this brought allowed Verdi in the next phase to work more slowly, but the years from about 1862 to 1878 were marked by crises in his personal relations, in his standing within the artistic life of his newly united country, in two great but awkward operas – what amounted almost to a 'male menopause'. The last phase is that of the evergreen, now somewhat pacified composer who – while the society he lived in did its best to freeze him into a national monument – completed one of his most original works in his eightieth year.

The book follows Verdi's life broadly through these phases. It now and then pursues a topic beyond the time when it first comes to notice. Verdi's exploitation of new copyright laws is one example; another is the process by which he bought, built up, and, over half a century, ran his landed estate. Both are more central to the composer's life than has often been acknowledged; both are easily lost sight of in the unfolding year by year of a mainly operatic career. In looking now and then at a single topic over a long span we run small risk of losing the thread of Verdi's individual development. The strength, at all points in his life, of his personality, and the determination with which he shaped his life's work, will see to that.

1 The innkeeper's son, 1813–1842: *Oberto* to *Nabucco*

According to a dubious story Verdi liked to tell, his mother, her five-month-old son clutched to her breast, hid in the village church tower from Russian troops which in the last months of the Napoleonic wars swept across northern Italy. What makes the story dubious is that early in 1814 the armies of several nations were fighting in the north Italian plain, but no Russians. The Russians – feared by country people in an area many invaders had plundered – were there, but in 1799–1800. Luigia Verdi probably did hide in the tower, and later mixed up two frightening experiences.

The story she told her son was none the less appropriate. Influences that were to shape his career and outlook sprang from the crucial years around the turn of the century. In 1796–97 young Napoleon Bonaparte's troops imposed French revolutionary ideals on Italy, a land far poorer and more backward than France; in 1799 the French armies fell back before the Russians and Austrians; in 1800–01 they reconquered most of the northern plain and held on to it. The republican governments they set up brought, for a time, the end of the old oligarchical rule in the eleven petty states that had divided the Italian peninsula.

For most people in and around the small town of Busseto, in the former duchy of Parma – as for many elsewhere – the truly notable change was the subduing of the Catholic Church to the new republics, bringing the confiscation and sale of Church lands. Together with the oppressiveness of French generals and officials it stirred resistance, at times violent, from the peasant bulk of the population, but it benefited a minority and helped to bind them to the new ideals.

The sale of Church lands benefited people already well off, like Antonio Barezzi, a merchant of Busseto who was to become Verdi's second father and then his father-in-law, rather than small landholders like his natural father Carlo Verdi, who kept an inn at Roncole, a village two and a half miles from the town. This is a general statement about classes: we do not know that Barezzi was a purchaser, though it seems likely enough. He went on admiring the Napoleonic regime (socially more conservative in its later, imperial phase) long after its overthrow in 1814. Under the restored duchy of Parma – a consolation prize for Napoleon's separated Austrian wife Marie-Louise – Barezzi and his kinsman Giuseppe Demaldè stood at the heart of a group of townspeople who, though not necessarily unbelievers, were hostile to priests. Carlo and Luigia Verdi, in contrast, were assiduous members of the Church flock. The dividing line between clericals and anticlericals – etched by the French Revolution throughout Latin Europe – ran between Giuseppe Verdi's two families. In opting for the Barezzis, people at the heart of Busseto musical life, he would in the first place obey the needs of a budding career, but he would also choose a set of ideals and a political stance.

Among musicians these years of turmoil identified some with the republican regime, some with the beleaguered Church. Ferdinando Provesi, who was to be Verdi's main teacher in his formative years, during the 1799–1801 period of Austro-Russian control was in forced residence for theft (from the treasury of the church where he was organist). At the return of the French in 1801 he fled to Busseto, where the protection of a rich family – not the Barezzis but equally close to the new regime – made him organist of the parish church and town music master; this meant ousting the incumbent, who had been Church-appointed and, probably, identified with the old regime. When in 1834 Verdi's candidature to succeed the dead Provesi brought a local 'civil war', it had deep roots.

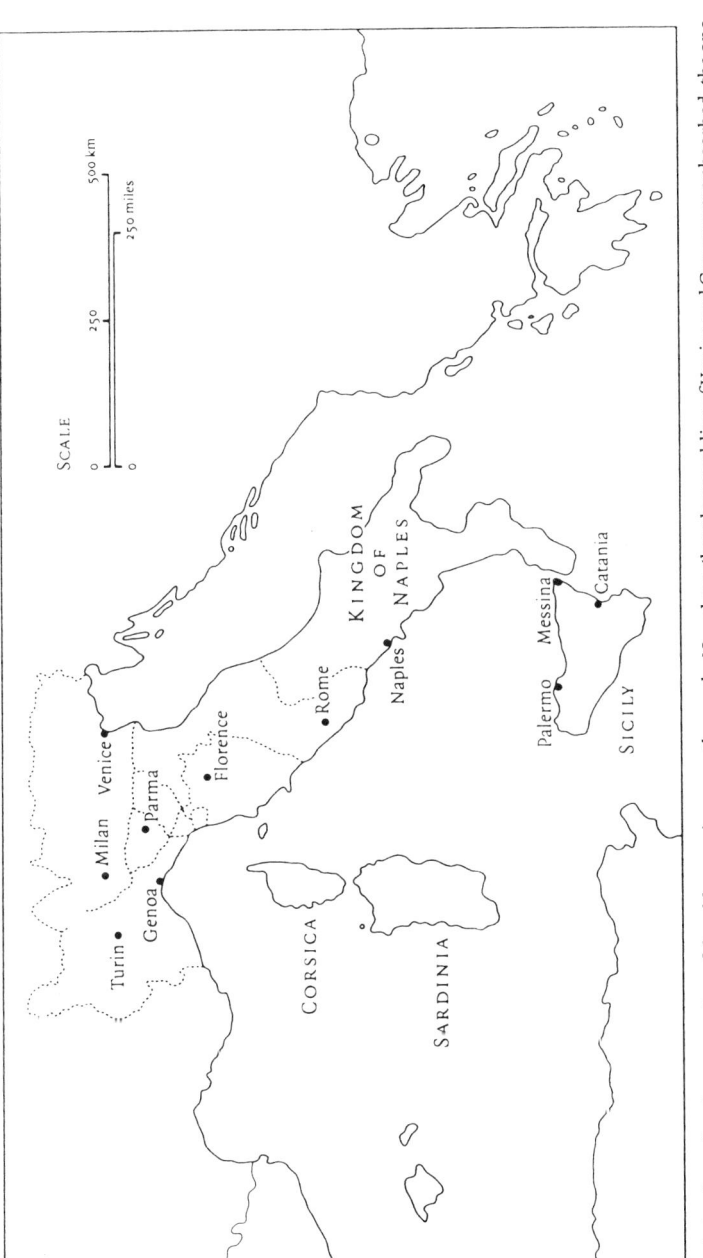

Italy in 1815, after the restoration of the old sovereigns overthrown by Napoleon (but the republics of Venice and Genoa were absorbed, the one into the Austrian-ruled kingdom of Lombardy-Venetia, the other into the Kingdom of Sardinia, ruled from Turin)

Nor was this the end of French influence. Shortly after his birth on 9 October 1813 – even this date is contested[1] – Carlo and Luigia Verdi's son was registered with the civil authorities as Joseph-François-Fortunin Verdi. He was in fact a French citizen: Napoleon as emperor had annexed to France about a third of the Italian mainland, Parma included. True, by 1813 the empire was tottering to its end. Meanwhile the cumulative effect of high taxes, conscription, and a stop on overseas trade, all aimed at furthering Napoleon's conquests, worsened the agricultural depression that settled on Europe for the next decade, on Italy for rather longer.

Giuseppe – the true version of his name – was the Verdis' first and, so far, only child; two and a half years later they had a daughter, Giuseppa, who was to die aged seventeen. The family's background and status are now well understood thanks to the researches of Mary Jane Phillips-Matz. In his later years Verdi made himself out to be a 'peasant from Roncole', 'totally ignorant' about music and with little knowledge of anything else: 'I am just a peasant, rough-hewn, and I have never been able to express an opinion worth twopence' (C, 176, 511, 616; VI, 26). This was in part a famous composer's defensive ploy, handy when someone badgered him for advice or tried to draw him into controversy. As an account of his origins and education it was literally untrue; in an exaggerated way it hinted at a larger truth.

His father's and his mother's families were much alike. Both were innkeepers and grocers who had moved to or within the Busseto neighbourhood around the turn of the century, the Verdis from Sant'Agata – about as far from the town as Roncole, but on the opposite, western side – the Uttinis from somewhat farther west; both were Lombard as the term was then understood, that is, inhabitants of the 'waveless plain' to the west of Mantua and Bologna, an area politically divided before and after Napoleonic rule among Milan, Parma, and Modena. Both families held parcels of land which they cultivated with hired labourers; around Roncole Carlo Verdi held on lease just over forty acres, while other Verdis farmed nearby or around Sant'Agata. The Uttinis, innkeepers in Busseto town, in the eighteenth century

1 The so-called birthplace at Roncole, near Busseto, in fact the inn where the boy Verdi grew up, from an old postcard

had numbered some priests and schoolteachers as well as some musicians; one, a minor composer, married a niece of the great composer Alessandro Scarlatti, but there is, alas, no direct line of descent from Scarlatti to Giuseppe Verdi.

Such families were a notable cut above the landless labourers who worked for them. Carlo Verdi lived at Roncole in a solid old farmhouse with nine rooms and outbuildings until, in 1830, years of agricultural depression and rent arrears led to his eviction; he then moved his inn to the so-called birthplace, a more modest house but no shack.[2] In a land of 90 per cent illiteracy he could write and keep accounts; was secretary and treasurer of the Roncole vestry; bought a spinet for his promising eight-year-old, a battered one which he had repaired; and sent Giuseppe to school, ultimately, at ten, to the gymnasium in Busseto, where the syllabus, based on the classics, was broadly like that of a contemporary grammar school in England. No peasant could have done it.

We should not, however, dismiss out of hand Verdi's account of his origins. Italy outside Milan had little to compare with the burgeoning middle classes of Britain and France. The Parma region, today, thanks to industrialisation, among the richest parts of Europe, was then as poverty-stricken as most of Italy; its people readily divided into *signori* ('ladies and gentlemen') and the rest, with only a peppering of lawyers, civil servants, doctors, and pharmacists – themselves nearly all minor landowners – between the nobility and the plebs. Carlo Verdi was not a labourer on the verge of starvation, but he was not the equivalent of a contemporary English farmer with two to three hundred acres, like Robert Martin in Jane Austen's *Emma*, a comfortable match for Harriet and beyond Emma's patronage; nor, assuredly, was he a *signore*. An important thread in Giuseppe's life was to be his climb to *signore* status.

In such a land, education was mostly in the hands of the clergy. Verdi's first teacher – he taught the boy privately from the age of four, then in the village school – was not a priest, but he sometimes played the organ in the Roncole parish church; musical and general schooling went hand in hand, and by the time the teacher died, the ten-year-old Giuseppe could take over at the organ, occasionally at first, full-time from the age of twelve.

He had meanwhile, aged about nine, started studying two or three times a week with a priest in Busseto, mostly Latin, mathematics, and Italian. The Italian was needed because, like nearly all members of his generation, Verdi grew up speaking dialect – one of those current from the Rhone to the Adriatic, with some French-sounding vowels: when he was eighty-five, a visitor from Turin noted that he still pronounced Italian with French 'u's, 'as our old people used to in Piedmont' (VB, 490). People like the Verdis could manage some Italian when they wrote letters or dealt with officialdom or with strangers to the area, but they had to work at it. The adult Giuseppe would write pungent Italian, with the odd error in the less usual subjunctive tense; his Latin schooling would show in a persistent habit of writing 'dumque' for the Italian 'dunque' ('therefore').

The decisive steps in his education came when he was aged ten to twelve. Starting at the gymnasium meant keeping school terms in Busseto: at first he lodged with a shoemaker's family, relatives of a neighbour; on Sundays he walked home to play the organ and visit his family; he also spent summers at Roncole. Working with the town music master Provesi, as he did from the age of twelve, meant embarking on his serious musical career. Both meant getting away from the Verdi family milieu. His schoolfellows were to go on to professional or official careers. The music-making – which Giuseppe concentrated on from the age of thirteen – shortly meant getting to know Antonio Barezzi and his family as far more than well-off patrons who had stood godparent to some of his relatives. By the time Verdi was seventeen he had become so much Barezzi's unofficially adopted son that he went to live in Barezzi's handsome town house. There was no breach: Carlo Verdi still signed official documents on his son's behalf, but the guiding influence was now Barezzi.

About Verdi's relations with his natural parents we know little. Accounts of his childhood at Roncole tell of a shy boy who did not mix

2 Antonio Barezzi, Verdi's 'second father' and father-in-law

much with his fellows or with anyone else, though he sometimes helped out at the inn. He seems to have remained close to his parents in feeling, to his mother in particular, while growing away from them in other ways. By the time the father died in 1867, Verdi's second wife wrote that she and her husband were both grief-stricken, though they had been 'at antipodes' from the old man 'in our ways of thinking'

(WalkerV, 268). At Barezzi's death later in the same year Verdi's grief was more explicit: 'if there is another life he will see whether I have loved him and whether I am grateful for all he did for me. He died in my arms and I have the solace of never having upset him' (*VI*, 79).

Anticlericalism was probably not the first tie between him and his second father. True, another story the mature Verdi liked to tell was of himself as a six-year-old altar boy being pushed by the angry priest so that he fell down the altar steps; the boy's dialect curse – 'May you die by lightning!' – came true eight years later. But that was most likely a passing episode.

What made Barezzi notice the adolescent Verdi was his musicmaking. Barezzi, described by his kinsman as a 'besotted amateur' musician, could play several instruments and was the chief mover in the town's philharmonic society; some of its concerts were held in his large music-room. At the heart of the northern plain, urban musical life revolved around several institutions – the opera house, the orchestra (often municipally subsidised) that played there, the main church, the town band, the philharmonic society, the town music school – but the same musicians often played, sang, or taught in each; the church organist might be the town music master and the chief répétiteur of the orchestra, where some of his students would play as unwaged apprentices. In a town like Busseto, too small to have a regular opera season, the philharmonic society was largely amateur; it made up both orchestra and band and some of its members played in church on the instruments allowed there.

Lack of regular seasons did not prevent Busseto's musical culture in the 1820s from being soaked in opera – available live in several larger towns not far off (the area from Milan to the Adriatic was the heartland of the genre), on paper in transcriptions published for 'besotted amateurs'. Church music, which still required some understanding of the 'learned' (contrapuntal) style, came a distant second. Military band music, propagated by a quarter-century of war, seeped into both theatre and church music as well as furnishing the staple of the town band. Viennese symphonic music as Haydn, Mozart, and Beethoven had developed it was nowhere.

Verdi's teacher Provesi was close to Barezzi both in music-making and in political stance. The boy gave his first concert at thirteen on the organ of the school chapel (replacing someone who was ill, and playing some of his own music); from the age of fourteen he composed for the philharmonic society's concerts; at sixteen he tried for, but did not get, a post as organist in another small town near by. In Holy Week 1830, when he was going on seventeen, he took the ailing Provesi's place in composing for a service, a procession, and a concert. This he did on the usual terms of unpaid apprenticeship – a way to keep the old man's salary going at a time when his post carried no pension; the tacit expectation was that Verdi would take over both salary and post at Provesi's death.

By then Verdi was spending so much time at the Barezzis' that he naturally fell in love with their daughter Margherita (his pupil for singing, only a few months younger) and she with him. Such were his 'shyness and reserve' that the Barezzi parents did not at first notice (A, 1, 75–6); when the mother did, she started chaperoning, but that did not prevent her and Antonio Barezzi from taking the young man into their house. They clearly thought of him as their future son-in-law and a musician with great expectations; they gave him a large, semi-independent room where he could work.

On the very day he moved in, Barezzi got him to petition the local authorities for a scholarship to study at the Milan Conservatorio, the music school founded by the Napoleonic government – an institution of higher calibre than anything the duchy of Parma could offer. We cannot readily tell what Verdi's musical achievements then were: he later wrote that he had destroyed many of the overtures, marches, cantatas, piano variations, and sacred music composed at Busseto. The small-town audience were perhaps content with fairly crude work, and with a less than prodigious display as executive musician; to learn the piano, an instrument new to Busseto, Verdi had had to teach himself from manuals. He was a local wonder, but no one suggested that as composer or player he was a prodigy by European standards, like the young Mozart.

Barezzi's move showed that he thought Verdi's future lay in opera, the form cultivated by every leading Italian composer and the aim of most Conservatorio students. That need not mean that the young man would desert Busseto. Opera composers often doubled as cathedral *maestri di cappella* (composer-organists), like Giovanni Gazzaniga and his successor Stefano Pavesi in their native Lombard town of Crema; Pavesi was still there. True, as church music declined in prestige such posts had come to look like something to retire to when a career in opera faltered; the reigning king of opera, Rossini, had never bothered with one. Verdi, however, might well have come back from Milan to a brilliant early spell in Busseto, with opera commissions starting to come his way; then, after the Italian composer's usual peripatetic career, on the move from one opera house to the next, he could have returned to a sunset period in the Busseto collegiate church, all to the greater glory of the town, the Barezzi network of friends and kin, and music.

To get a modest scholarship (of 300 francs – £12 – a year for four years) turned out difficult. The local charitable foundation called the Monte di Pietà gave out four a year, but they were pledged for two and a half years ahead; a further petition to the government at Parma brought only approval for Verdi's taking the first vacancy. In the end Barezzi anticipated the first year's payment: Verdi left for Milan in June 1832.

There he failed the entrance examination to the Conservatorio. The reasons for his failure are now well understood. As Verdi himself owned in the application he signed at the time, he was an over-age 'foreigner' and needed to have an exception made. The chief trouble was that the piano teacher thought the position of his hands all wrong: at eighteen he was – the man said – too old to learn. The director and his deputy, after looking over Verdi's compositions, opined that if further study of counterpoint disciplined his 'genuine imagination' he would do well, but in a school already overcrowded the case for exceptional treatment had not been made. It was an understandable conclusion, though Verdi was to resent it all his life; he kept the official letter of rejection prominent among his papers.

For Barezzi this was an emergency. There are hints from the

Bussetan teacher with whom Verdi lodged in Milan that the young man's failure might have looked like a reverse for the anticlerical faction back home. The answer was for Verdi to study privately in Milan with Vincenzo Lavigna, a learned sixty-six-year-old composer and répétiteur who had at one time enjoyed mild success in opera. This, however, meant that Barezzi had to spend perhaps three times what he had expected. Almost at once he had to pay not just for the lessons and Verdi's room and board but for a bed, a suit of clothes, a square piano, music paper, a subscription to La Scala (presumably to the stalls or orchestra, then a relatively cheap part of the house where you stood or sat on unnumbered benches). It is a measure of Barezzi's faith in Verdi and his open-heartedness that he demurred – gently – only in 1835, by which time Verdi was living on his own, neglecting his teacher (probably outgrown), and spending more than he had as a lodger. Barezzi was testier with the Monte di Pietà, which would repay him the scholarship money he had advanced only after a long bureaucratic wrangle.

Verdi spent the three years until July 1835 in Milan, going home for a short summer holiday in 1833 and a six-month break in the latter half of 1834. His failure to enter the Conservatorio was a blessing in disguise. As a pupil he would have had to wear uniform and spend all his time with fellow music students. Instrumental practice would have taken up far more of the day than Lavigna could enforce. Verdi might well have emerged as a finished musician, with little knowledge of anything outside music. Instead he had the resources of Milan open to him – true, to be enjoyed on doled-out pocket money. The wide interests he later showed suggest that he drew from those resources all he could, unlike other Italian composers of the time, whose world began and pretty well ended with opera.

As the capital of Napoleon's kingdom of Italy (a misnomer, for 'Italy' included only a north-eastern wedge of the peninsula) Milan had developed a solid middle class of officials and professional people, with a sprinkling of merchants, bankers, and manufacturers. Under the successor kingdom of Lombardy-Venetia, a possession of

Austria, this middle class was to grow dangerously out of step with the 'suitable' jobs open to it – a chief cause of the aspirations and disturbances known collectively as the Risorgimento. Meanwhile the city, overcrowded within its still extant walls, was the intellectual and operatic capital of Italy. Its bookseller-publishers, and their readers, were the liveliest in a country where few people read. La Scala was now the leading Italian opera house, as it had not been in the eighteenth century; four other, more modest theatres gave opera at least part of the time. As in the rest of Italy, a government made fearful by the French Revolution allowed no political debate; a flourishing crop of journals therefore dealt in the first place with opera, a topic not only safe but of absorbing interest, for the works of Rossini, Bellini, and Donizetti had given the genre a fresh, intense appeal. More news of opera went round the cafés – for men, a hub of social life.

How much of all this Verdi took in we do not know. His lifelong habit of theatregoing – not only to opera, and in Milan not just to La Scala – clearly started then; it may have taught him as much as his formal lessons. So may his habit of reading books unrelated to music, novels and plays in particular; even bad novels could open his mind to something other than musical routine (in the trough of depression after his wife's death a few years later he was to gulp down one after another). He already knew some modern Italian literature such as Manzoni's great historical novel *The Betrothed*; now he was exposed to the French Romantics and, in translation, to more exotic writers like Byron and Schiller. In Milan, French intellectual influence was strong. When Verdi mastered his generally good French is not clear; he was to take lessons in it in 1846, but may have begun to pick it up here: educated Milanese readily spoke the language, not too difficult for a northern Italian. Verdi's self-education was far from systematic; it none the less made him unlike the run of Italian musicians, who held to an artisan tradition and outlook.

His personal life is still more obscure. After fifteen months, his landlord the Bussetan teacher began to complain of 'boorish manners'; he eventually insisted on Verdi's moving to other lodgings, told Barezzi that he wished he had never set eyes on the young man, spoke of his gallivanting too much about town, and hinted at unmentionable behaviour – probably to do with his own daughter. Verdi, who in later years referred to himself as a 'bear', was not a smooth or ingratiating person. His landlord, though, sounds very ready to take offence; he was to relent later on, but only after Verdi was safely married.

Lavigna's formal teaching as Verdi later recalled it consisted almost exclusively of making him work at counterpoint and fugue: the old man, trained in the eighteenth-century Neapolitan school, insisted that the only good model for composition was the Naples master Paisiello, often upheld by conservatives who set his tuneful simplicity against Rossini's 'noisy' innovations; Verdi therefore stopped showing him his own – unPaisiellian – work. This is not the whole truth: Lavigna did set him to 'ideal composition', presumably free-ranging in a modern idiom.

Verdi studied some of Corelli's string sonatas; to judge from his later advice on a curriculum for music students, he probably worked on other late seventeenth- and eighteenth-century Italian music (by Alessandro Scarlatti, Durante, Leo, Marcello). His repeated avowals of musical 'ignorance' in later life do not square with the contents of the library he then possessed, which held a wide variety of music old and new, from Palestrina to Wagner; nor does his statement to a friend that he 'did not take in' music by reading a score (C, 618). The mature Verdi, however, drew a line between his admitted knowledge of counterpoint and musical 'erudition', which he disclaimed. No doubt, too, he had only gradually come to know a wide range of music outside the Italian school; though Milan underwent some Austrian cultural influence, the Viennese classics were, if anything, less cultivated there in the 1830s than they had been twenty years earlier. In that sense Verdi was self-taught and, like many such, prickly about his want of academic training.

One Viennese work Milan did cultivate was Haydn's *Creation*. It was put on in April 1834 by the philharmonic society, a body largely amateur but far grander and, no doubt, more proficient than its Busseto namesake: it included members of the most exalted noble families, one of whom was later to sing the bass solo in the first Italian performance of Rossini's Stabat Mater. Verdi, by his own later account, got the répétiteur's job because he was the only person at hand willing to accompany from the full score:

> I remember very well the ironical smiles of some of the amateur ladies and gentlemen, and it seems that my youthful figure, lean and not too tidily dressed, was not such as to inspire much confidence [. . .] little by little warming up and getting excited, instead of confining myself to accompanying, I began also to conduct with my right hand [. . .] I had a great success – all the greater for being unexpected. (Walker V, 16–17)

This led to further work – unpaid. Verdi hoped that friendship with the society's director, Pietro Massini, might bring an opera commission; Massini got as far as putting him on to two librettists in turn.

Nine months before the *Creation* performance Verdi's old teacher Ferdinando Provesi had died. The result was the Busseto 'civil war' over the proposed appointment of Verdi to succeed him, an event not unique in the Lombard plain – another small town, Guastalla, was riven a few years later by a struggle over a like appointment – but uniquely well documented.

North Italian towns were close-knit both physically and socially. Factional struggles, when they blew up, sundered people, perhaps related, who ran across each other in the street and knew all too much about one another's past; those who clung together might develop a fierce group loyalty. Quarrels often arose between the supporters of rival opera singers or ballet dancers – at Piacenza in 1824, at Reggio in 1841, at Parma in 1843, all within easy reach of Busseto; so violent were the Reggio disturbances that the government expelled some nobles from the town and cut the opera season short. The evidence is fragmentary, but where political debate was banned ructions of this kind most likely gave vent to long-standing enmity between clerical conservatives and anticlerical liberals. The Busseto 'war' clearly did: Barezzi's kinsman Giuseppe Demaldè compared the provost of the collegiate church – leader of the clerical party – to the Spanish Inquisition; the provost and his supporters were almost certainly getting their own back more than thirty years after the French-inspired republic had imposed on the church the 'Jacobin' Provesi.

For nearly a year after the *maestro di cappella*'s death Barezzi and his group held off: they needed to wait until Verdi completed his studies or at least could turn up with a good reference from his teacher. They expected a competition to be held for the organist's post, which Verdi would win; the Monte di Pietà and the municipality would round off the salary by appointing him town music master as well. That was why Verdi returned to Busseto on 20 June 1834. Two days earlier, however, the provost had played his trump: the vestry of the collegiate church appointed Giovanni Ferrari, an 'outsider', organist without a competition.

Rumours and recriminations flew about; both sides tried to enlist the Monte di Pietà; Verdi and his supporters appealed to the government at Parma to impose a competition; the philharmonic society decided to stop playing in church services; violence broke out – a fist fight in church at Christmas; for fear of worse, the government at length banned instrumental music (other than organ) in the Busseto churches. A complicating factor was the belief that Verdi was now wrapped up in opera and intended to move to Milan as soon as possible: the mayor quoted the young man's unofficial fiancée Margherita Barezzi to that effect. This may have been true, but Verdi, enmeshed in obligations to Barezzi and his party, could not back out of the local struggle: when it had been going for nearly eighteen months he was tempted by a competition for a cathedral post at Monza – a larger town, close to Milan, that offered a better salary – but gave it up on Barezzi's account.

Bureaucratic slowness gave local enmities full play; the factions had time to mount rival concerts in some of which the Barezzi group used Verdi's works as ammunition. Only in January 1835 did Parma officialdom deliver a Solomonic judgment: the posts of organist and town music master-cum-director of the philharmonic society would be split; only the latter would be appointed by competition; Ferrari would stay. By then Verdi had gone back to Milan for a final, rather desultory seven months' study (and, perhaps, less desultory work on an opera). Only in February 1836 was the examination held – Verdi won easily; Ferrari did not enter – and only on 5 March was he appointed, to only half of Provesi's old job and at the measly salary of 657 francs (£26) a year.

When it was all over Verdi claimed, in a letter to the local authority, to have been 'an impassive spectator of this long struggle' (A, I, 222). This was untrue. He may by then have had enough of it; awareness of having been caught up in the affair as Barezzi's 'creature' at once embittered him against the town and the clergy and built up the determination, clear in his later life, to be independent of all comers. At the height of the 'war', though, he had – in letters to his own supporter Demaldè – called Ferrari 'low and malicious' (A, I, 199) and the provost 'a monstrous, black soul'.[3] As late as 1853, Busseto's failure to appoint his disciple Emanuele Muzio, a local man, would rouse him to denounce 'these pricks of priests, who would not have me as maestro here' (A, II, 240).[4]

Verdi signed on 20 April 1836 a nine-year contract to be town music master, renewable every three years. Four days earlier he and Margherita Barezzi had been formally betrothed; on 4 May they were married. The job meant giving five individual lessons a week to, at one time, as many as thirteen young Bussetans, besides composing and directing rehearsals for the philharmonic society, with two months' holiday a year. No wonder that after six months Verdi asked whether the Monza post was still open – he was 'wasting' his youth in a place far from Milan that gave 'no hope of advancement'[5] – or that he resigned as soon as his contract allowed, three years later, even though his prospects at that time were still uncertain; in his letter to the mayor he pointedly regretted not having been as useful as he wished to 'this most unhappy town of mine' (A, I, 250).

3 Margherita Barezzi, Verdi's first wife. Oil painting by Augusto Mussini

The marriage remains one of the private areas in Verdi's life; Margherita Verdi is scarcely more than a name. Her portraits depict a hairdo elaborate even for the 1830s, but multiple coils and diadem surround a face that tells one little. After a honeymoon trip to Milan the young couple – both twenty-two – settled in a good flat in Busseto, necessarily paid for by the bride's father. A daughter, Virginia, was born on 26 March 1837, a son, Icilio Romano, on 11 July 1838; their names – those of Roman Republican martyrs, victims of a tyrant – had clear political connotations. Each was to die when just over a year old, as many children did in times before the causes of infection were known. Margherita Verdi followed in June 1840, eight months after the son she had been unable to breastfeed. The cause entered in the death register, rheumatic fever, leaves sufferers open to infection. A later writer who interviewed Verdi talked of 'inflammation of the brain': she may have died of meningitis.

This brief, death-blasted period of family life was intertwined with Verdi's making his way into opera. The Busseto philharmonic society played his overtures and other works, he published nine songs in 1838–39, but *Oberto, conte di San Bonifacio* was the first work to bring him before a large public. After a relatively long period of gestation it was performed at La Scala on 17 November 1839, met with fair success among both audience and critics, had fourteen performances that season, and was revived in Turin and, again, at La Scala the following year. Verdi had not exactly arrived, but he was now a man to watch.

For a leading opera house to put on a work by a beginner is today inconceivable; a new opera by a well-known composer – given now and then as a duty – is enough of a risk, and may well mean a thin house. Matters were quite different when Verdi set out. Operas in leading Italian theatres were by definition new or recent; during the 1830s La Scala gave thirty-eight new operas, more than in any decade before or since. As a system of production Italian opera was closer to 1930s Hollywood cinema or present-day television than to the museum art that opera has largely become. New works had to come forward all the time, some unavoidably by new composers. Of these, some would fail and be at once withdrawn, some (often the same ones) would be put on at the composer's expense, but now and again the impresario had to take a chance on an untried artist who could not afford to pay and who, on the contrary, had to be offered something – like a half-share in publishing rights that could be sold only if the work was a success.

That was how Bartolomeo Merelli came to put on *Oberto*. A vain, ambitious man who had started as an agent and librettist and who provided opera companies for a network of theatres in northern Italy and Vienna, he had managed La Scala since 1829, at first in partnership, now in sole charge. Such a figure had many collaborators and acquaintances who would put a promising artist in his way. It would help if the artist could be in Milan, attracting notice with other kinds of work; hence Verdi's frustration at having to remain in Busseto. As it was, he seems to have become known to the impresario chiefly through Massini, the director of the Milan philharmonic society, and through the journalist Antonio Piazza, who wrote him a libretto at Massini's instance.

All through 1836 and then off and on through the next two years Verdi was at work on an opera. Whether it was always the same one has long exercised scholars. In a sense the question is idle: an opera, like a film script, did not exist until it was produced, and then it had to fit the particular singers engaged; even when *Oberto* came forward Verdi had to revise it for a new cast, and again for later seasons. There certainly was an earlier *Rochester* (Verdi spelt it without an 'h'), more or less based on the Restoration poet and rake, some of which got into *Oberto*; there may have been a *Lord Hamilton* (Tudor–Stuart history was a popular source, at once lurid and helpfully remote).

Verdi at first (1836–37) had hopes of a production at Parma or Piacenza, the two chief towns of the duchy, and later at what may have been a second-rank Milan theatre; any of these would have been a more normal goal for a beginner than La Scala, 'the first theatre in the world' as Verdi called it – the kind of alleged supremacy he would mock in later years, whether claimed for Milan, Paris, or Naples (WalkerV, 27). By November 1837, however, the Parma impresario – financially straitened and in no mood to take risks – had rebuffed him; he therefore asked his Milan connections, Massini and Piazza, to try Merelli.

Something came of this, and of two trips Verdi made to Milan in the spring and autumn of 1838. By the second trip his hopes were firm enough for him to give up the Busseto post on his return, and to move to Milan in February 1839 with his wife and surviving child – this though the earlier trips and the family's expenses in Milan, right up to the first performance of *Oberto*, depended on loans from Barezzi and other Busseto relatives and friends. Of one such loan Verdi wrote to Barezzi that his hope was 'certainly not [that] of accumulating wealth, but that of amounting to something among men' (A, I, 315).

Opera house schedules were easily disrupted by the unlooked-for. Merelli thought of giving *Oberto* in spring 1839, with three of the finest singers of the day, the soprano Giuseppina Strepponi, the tenor Napoleone Moriani, and the baritone Giorgio Ronconi, but Moriani's illness prevented it; Strepponi, years later Verdi's lover and then his wife, and Ronconi, the future creator of Nabucco, may have encouraged the impresario to go ahead with the work, but that was as much as they had to do with the new composer. They then left for other theatres; Verdi had to adapt his opera to the different vocal ranges of the less starry mezzo-soprano and bass engaged for the autumn season. Merelli brought in Temistocle Solera to tinker with Piazza's libretto, and got Verdi to write a new quartet, its slow section one of the finest things in the work.

Not that *Oberto* was a masterpiece even by the uncertain lights of Italian opera in 1839. Rossini had dropped out ten years earlier; Bellini was dead; Donizetti had gone to Paris. Mercadante, it is true, had been composing reform operas of interestingly new cut; with many virtues, they lacked memorable tunes and were not great hits. The moment was one of transition. Just what it was transiting towards Verdi was to make blazingly clear less than three years later; meanwhile he followed, at times halted, in the steps of his predecessors. The lion-breath that told of things to come blew only here and there, in reflective moments like the grandly hewn slow section of the Act I finale. The work is not boring: the flow of rhythmic energy is already too high for that. But if it were not by Verdi *Oberto* would scarcely be remembered.

The obvious thing for Merelli to do was to give Verdi a contract for more operas. The first, for the autumn 1840 season, was to have been a serious work, but the theatre's needs as the impresario saw them changed and he asked Verdi for a comic opera. The genre was in decline, at odds with the earnest mood of the Romantic age. Significantly, the best libretto Verdi could find was twenty-two years old. Un giorno di regno – the new title given the partly revised text – would have suited Rossini; much of the music Verdi wrote on it sounds like Rossini without the fizz. It might have done so even if he had not had to compose under dire stress: soon after he had begun, Margherita Verdi died. At twenty-six he was left alone.

What happened to Verdi between his wife's death on 18 June 1840 and the triumphant first night of Nabucco on 9 March 1842 is still unclear. His own accounts, given to two biographers many years later (in 1869 and 1881), are contradictory and in some ways wrong. Yet, as with other inaccurate statements by Verdi, they seem to embody a basic truth. The trouble, we may guess, is in large part his unconscious need to dramatise: a crucial conversation takes place on a snowy night in Milan (which probably did not take place then, or in that form); when in deepest dejection he lets the unknown libretto fall and his eye lights on a revelatory passage (a different one in each of the two accounts); and so on.

That Verdi was shattered by the loss of his wife and children is beyond doubt. On a short visit to Busseto he struck his wife's kinsman Demaldè as wanting only 'to hide in some dark place and live out his miserable existence'.[6] The wound would never quite heal: over a decade later, when people objected to the multiple deaths in Trovatore he retorted 'after all, in life all is death! What exists? . . .'; in his seventies he would write over and over – prompted by the death of a friend's loved one – 'life is sorrow', 'life is the stupidest thing, and worse still, it's pointless', 'misfortune rules the world'. He came to believe in 'fate' – and fate was not benign (C, 503, 505, 506, 530, 532).

Nor could he quite purge his grief in creative work. The high point of a Verdi opera – many have noticed – is often a duet between father and daughter. Some duets show them in conflict, like Amonasro and

Aida; others are consolatory – a strong father or father figure sustains a young woman mired in deep distress, as in Giovanna d'Arco, Luisa Miller, Rigoletto, Traviata. One scene cuts so near the bone as to hint that for its sake Verdi may have chosen the libretto of Simon Boccanegra, obscurities and all: the child who vanished in infancy turns out, twenty years later, to be miraculously alive; she and Simone recognise one another in a duet of poignant lyrical beauty; in the council chamber scene added to the 1881 revised version her great arching phrase pours blessing on her father's plea for brotherhood and peace. Yet 'misfortune rules the world' and other black views of existence postdate even this late work.

Meanwhile, in the summer of 1840, the impresario needed the score of Un giorno di regno; he insisted on Verdi's finishing it. Having to work, and work fast, could have been therapeutic even though the strain set up the first of many throat ailments. Unhappily the first night was also the last. The singers were unwell or tired; the work was mediocre but – as Verdi, still smarting, wrote nearly twenty years later – no worse than some that had been tolerated or even liked; the audience hissed; it 'ill-treated the work of a poor sick young man, pressed for time and with his heart broken by a ghastly misfortune! All this was known [. . .] Oh, if the audience had – I won't say applauded, but silently borne with that opera, I shouldn't have words enough to thank them!' As it was – the now hugely successful composer added – 'I accept hisses, on condition that I shouldn't be asked to give thanks for applause' (C, 556–7).

Verdi's story that the failure made him want to give up his career does not square with the work he did on Oberto in the autumn of 1840 and the following winter; he probably helped to rehearse it for its further successful run at La Scala, and then composed at least one new number for a production at Genoa. It is probably true that Merelli declined to quarrel with him and – whether on a snowy night or not – put him on to Solera's libretto Nabucodonosor (later Nabucco), remotely based on the biblical story of Nebuchadnezzar, closer at hand on a recent ballet; true too that Verdi was fired by the possibilities of the

4 Verdi about the time of his breakthrough with *Nabucco*, 1842. Anonymous lithograph

text. The basic story – Merelli eased a promising young artist out of his deep depression – seems likely enough.

Verdi composed Nabucco sometime in 1841 and had it ready in the autumn. His story of disputes with Merelli over the date of the first performance is odd, because Nabucco was an obvious candidate for the season when it was in fact given, namely Lent: that was when Italian theatres gave 'sacred dramas' (operas based on biblical themes), though they no longer, as in the eighteenth century, had to confine themselves to such works. Rossini's Mosè in Egitto, the model for Nabucco, had been put on in Lent 1818 as a 'sacred drama'.[7]

This time Verdi had the boon of the great baritone Giorgio Ronconi in the title part and the fine French bass Prosper Dérivis as the Jewish leader Zaccaria. Giuseppina Strepponi – who again liked the young composer's music – in the exacting part of Abigaille was far from a boon: as she tended to, she rushed to Milan part way through the season from an engagement elsewhere; for that and other reasons she was in desperate vocal health. The first performance was none the less an overwhelming success. Offers poured in from managers, invitations from ladies of the aristocracy. A new voice had broken through; Verdi was made.

2 The galley slave, 1842–1847: *Nabucco* to *Macbeth*

'Since *Nabucco* one may say I've never had an hour's peace. Sixteen years in the galleys!' So Verdi wrote in 1858 to his long-standing friend and admirer Countess Clarina Maffei (C, 572).

He had just completed *Un ballo in maschera*, his twenty-third opera, but the hazards that dogged the making of such a work – specially awkward this time – had kept him from hearing it performed. When, a year later, *Ballo* at length reached the stage Verdi regarded it as a landmark. Never again would he suffer the old work rhythm, to his mind so like that of a galley slave pulling at the oar; never again would he deal direct with impresarios and the sleazy theatre world they stood for. In the remaining four decades of his life he was to write just five new operas.

Brooding, after one more year, over the hard-won success of *Ballo* and his own indifference to it, Verdi wrote to the librettist he most often worked with, Francesco Maria Piave:

> I have adored and still adore this art [of music], and when I'm struggling on my own with my notes my heart pounds, tears well from my eyes and I'm moved and delighted beyond telling, but if I think that these poor notes of mine have to be thrown to unintelligent creatures, to a publisher who sells them for the entertainment or the contempt of the masses, then I no longer love anything! . . . Let's not talk about it. (CV, II, 353–4)

The Romantic artist – we seem to hear – marks himself off from having to cater for a world ruled by modern business values. In practice Verdi made those values his own and met their demands – at a cost. Unlike Berlioz, who could never impose his vision on the audience or the managers of the Paris Opéra, Verdi by 1860 was the most successful opera composer of the age; at most, five or six of his works had failed to go beyond a few Italian theatres, but all the others had been immediate hits and some were performed literally round the world. Surely – to all appearances – if ever an artist was integrated into the system of production he worked for, Verdi was he.

Nor did the galley slave's work rate equal that of some fellow-composers. Donizetti and the now forgotten Pacini turned out on average three to four operas a year. The Italian opera circuit imposed this rhythm of production or something close to it: all the leading theatres expected to put on new works in each of the three main seasons (carnival – stretching from Boxing Day to sometime in late February or March – spring, and autumn). Like the impresarios who managed each season on behalf of the theatre owners, the singers who performed the new works, and the designers who clothed them in sets and costumes as resplendent as the manager could afford, composers expected to move about from one city and theatre to the next; they would be rehearsing and finishing one opera while they planned another and negotiated for a third. True, Bellini in his short career (1826–35) had composed on average just one opera a year; he had achieved almost at once the highest fees of any Italian composer, but that was because contemporaries acknowledged his talent as special.

Judged by this money standard – which he, like others, accepted – Verdi attained pre-eminence more slowly: only with *Macbeth* (1847), his tenth opera, did he trump Bellini's highest fee. At slightly less than two operas a year his average work rate fell between Bellini's and Donizetti's: in the seven years 1842–49, his busiest period, he wrote twelve new operas and one major revision. He was, all the same, closer to Bellini in regarding himself as an artist rather than a craftsman.

This showed in a number of ways. Rossini at the time of *The Barber of Seville* (1816) had done the traditional thing: he had stayed at the impresario's house and composed much of the work with the company laughing and talking around him. Verdi, however, declined to lodge with the impresario and stayed in hotels. After the first few operas he followed Bellini rather than the craftsmanlike Donizetti in preferring not to adjust his works to new voices unless sporadically; till then 'adjustment' had been a common task in an operatic world dominated by singers, who might alter or interpolate arias to suit themselves. Soon, when changes in the law made it possible, Verdi would insist on his operas' being performed as written.

In the 1840s it was still the composer's task to rehearse the company and direct the first three performances from the keyboard (there was no conductor in the modern sense: the leader normally took charge from the first violin desk). Verdi did not spare himself. His pupil and amanuensis Emanuele Muzio described him at a rehearsal of *I Lombardi alla prima crociata* (1843), his next opera after *Nabucco*: 'He shouts like a desperate man, stamps his feet as though he were playing the pedals on the organ, sweats so that drops fall on the score.'[1] Half a century later, the eighty-one-year-old Verdi, then rehearsing *Falstaff* in Paris, was still being described as a 'dynamo' and a 'force of nature' (IEV, 252). Neither early nor late did he mix much with the company, save now and again away from the theatre; until he felt the need to jump up and cajole or instruct the performers he remained seated 'with his great hands resting on his knees, motionless, like some Assyrian god' (IEV, 61). Among fellow-professionals he had little or no small talk.

The effort Verdi had to put forth to meet the demands of the Italian opera system showed above all in ill health. All through the 1840s and 1850s composing an opera brought on recurrent sore throats and stomach pains. The worst troubles came in 1845–46 when he had to compose three operas in quick succession for each of the three leading Italian opera houses: *Giovanna d'Arco* for La Scala, *Alzira* for the San Carlo in Naples, and *Attila* for La Fenice in Venice. These illnesses

– we know from Muzio – were real. The matter was sensitive because, in the hard-pressed world of Italian opera, managers and artists at times used illness as a pretext; medical certificates were not too hard to come by; Verdi himself may have exaggerated his 1845 troubles to avoid writing the part of Alzira for a singer he distrusted. We cannot check his later statement that he had been 'almost dying' when he completed *Attila* early in 1846, but he undoubtedly suffered a breakdown, lost much weight, and was ordered to rest (C, 108). Even after a period of idleness, work on *Macbeth* in late 1846 – an opera by which he set much store – brought on further intestinal pains and diarrhoea.

Here was a man who lived to be eighty-seven; once freed from the pressures of these early decades, he seems until his last three or four years to have enjoyed rude health. The sore throats and stomach pains were no doubt psychosomatic – and no less real for that. A like symptom was a low fever accompanied by depression – bad enough in Venice, where in January–February 1844 he was composing *Ernani*, to plunge him into 'despair' at nightfall; if the opera failed he would shoot out his brains, though when it turned out a hit the mood swung round and he found himself enjoying a city he had previously disliked (BM, 119–20).

It cannot have helped that, when engaged on an opera, Verdi might compose from 5 a.m. to 6 p.m. on a stomach empty but for repeated cups of coffee; on *Macbeth* he worked from 9 a.m. to midnight with only one break for dinner. Once the immediate task was over he would seek a cure by taking the waters at one or other Italian spa, a habit he kept up in later years when it was a pretext for a holiday. In the 1840s the waters only palliated the strain. No wonder he talked in April 1845 of writing just six more operas 'and then *goodbye* to all that' (A, I, 542).

The immense success of *Nabucco* – seventy-five performances at La Scala alone by the end of 1842 – launched Verdi into the upper-class social life of Milan, the city where he made his base. A naive account by his pupil Muzio shows him, when resting in 1846, 'always out and surrounded by noble satellites who seem unable to do without him'; besides inviting him to their houses they would send their carriages to take him into the country.² Friendships sprang up with several noblewomen, some older than Verdi, to whom he addressed letters of heavy-footed gallantry. The truest friend among them was Clarina Maffei. She and her husband, the poet Andrea Maffei, were amicably separated and she had a new companion; both Maffeis remained close to Verdi for many years.

Such close friendship – it has been well said – called for 'an attitude of intense respect and devotion [. . .] Given it, [Verdi] would relax his severity and treat with a kind of laughing indulgence the weaknesses of natures less adamantine than his own' (WalkerV, 301).

Whatever he did was, for Clarina Maffei, well done; after thirty years' friendship she would write that time had 'done nothing but add to your great mind experience, knowledge, depth of feeling' (CV, II, 296–7). Her husband wrote of Verdi's 'adamantine temper': it allowed the composer to fend off setting to music a song of Maffei's, though he himself – Maffei added – would, if asked, write on Verdi's old boots (WalkerV, 125). Another nobleman for whom Verdi could do no wrong was his long-time correspondent Count Opprandino Arrivabene; Verdi's many letters used him as a sounding-board.

Much the same was true of Verdi's few close friends in the world of opera. Muzio, his only long-standing pupil, was a young compatriot (from another village outside Busseto) who achieved a modest career as composer and a better one as conductor, mainly in the United States. All his life he showed doglike fidelity to his teacher-hero. 'The maestro', he reported to Antonio Barezzi, 'tells me at the start of the lesson: *remember that I am inexorable*; just imagine how that scares me; but my fear is dispelled bit by bit when he says *fine* [. . .] he won't let through a note that's just passable; he wants everything perfect.'³ Piave, now regarded by many as Verdi's ideal (because most subservient) librettist, was a beginner when they met in Venice in the winter of 1843–44. In this, his native city, the young man became Verdi's boon companion. Only to him, so far as we know, did Verdi write in the slangy, at times bawdy style used by many theatre people; a favourite form of address was 'Mr Cunt'. Verdi showed affectionate contempt; Piave by and large took it on the chin.

The one person who was at times to stand up to Verdi while remaining close to him, his second wife Giuseppina Strepponi, appears to have been for most of the 1840s no more than a friend – one whose faltering career took her for long periods away from places where they might have met. Though the evidence establishes nothing for sure, Frank Walker has convincingly argued from it that only in Paris in the winter of 1847–48 did they become lovers.

Meanwhile Verdi's time in Venice, Rome, Naples, Florence, and London – places where he had to finish an opera and see it onto the stage – was busier still than life at his home lodgings in Milan, all the more because of his habit of writing out most of the instrumentation during rehearsals. After *Nabucco* he was famous. It irked him to be stared at and gossiped about, a trial that seems to have been at its worst in Naples in 1845: what did it matter to the Neapolitans, he wrote three years later to the local impresario, if he went to a leading café, wore brown shoes rather than black, or was seen on the prima donna's balcony? He disclaimed any star narcissism: 'I am extremely frank, decisive, at times irascible, rough if you like, but never difficult or finicky, and if I seem so that is due not to me but to circumstances' (C, 57–8).

A man in his thirties whose looks and output suggested, above all, vigorous masculinity might be expected to have had a sexual life to match. Later, when he was fifty-two, a caricature statuette by a Paris artist showed Verdi as a lion seated at the piano, with his tail passing between his legs to play on the keyboard alongside one paw, while the other paw composed operas. Verdi reported the statuette to a friend as plain funny, and kept it in his house; he may have been unaware that in French slang 'queue' ('tail') means 'penis' (VI, 69).

About the reality we have no more than hints. After seasons in Venice in 1844 and 1851 the composer wrote jokingly to Piave about a certain 'angel' and – perhaps the same person – a 'Sior Toni' who in spite of the 'Sior' ('Mr') was a woman. In 1851 'Toni' threatened to come to Busseto, though she knew Verdi was living there with Strepponi; Strepponi herself a couple of years later joked about Piave's 'erotic zeal' when squiring her lover round Venice. There were

5 Caricature statuette of Verdi by Dantan Jeune, 1866. The original is at Sant'Agata

also Venetian 'lionesses' to be greeted – fashionable women (A, I, 129–30, 503, 513; BM, 257 (note); WalkerV, 104). The chances are that with one or other of these women, in Venice or elsewhere, the young widower had a fling – of no great moment.

His attitude to sex showed when he and Piave left out of *Rigoletto* the notorious scene in Victor Hugo's original play (the censorship, he knew, would never allow it). The king pulls out a key and lets himself into the room where the jester's kidnapped daughter is held; he has previously won her love while disguised as a student. When Verdi later refused to put in an extra aria for a prima donna, he made out that the only place for it would be the resulting bedroom encounter; a volley of exclamation marks showed how unthinkable that was. While he was writing the opera for Venice, however, he had agreed to drop the business of the key with the remark to Piave 'Oh Lord! These are simple, natural matters but the Patriarch [the head of the Catholic Church in Venice] can no longer relish the thought!'[4] 'Simple, natural' – a view no doubt more widely held in the mid nineteenth century than public attitudes of the time suggest. The age of the licensed brothel as the Latin male's hygienic exercise ground was about to start.

Not that the young Verdi (or indeed the older one) was an erotic artist. His works gave matchless voice to love as a passion – with almost no hint of sensuality. Even so seductive an appeal as Charles V's 'Vieni meco, sol di rose' in *Ernani* has an urgency not to be found in its nearest model, the stepped, winding, insinuating melody of Bellini. Love in Verdi's operas, besides, is as often that of parent and child, of friends, or of country as it is the mutual love of young men and women. Nor is 'love interest' always central to them. *Nabucco* makes little of it; there and in the next two Milan operas, *Lombardi* and *Giovanna d'Arco*, the dominant mood is of heroic, slightly crazed grandeur interspersed with lightning discharges of energy; *I due Foscari* (Rome, 1844) and *Macbeth* (Florence, 1847) do without a conventional love story.

The audiences that awarded *Nabucco* and its creator immediate fame found in the work a new experience. A driving energy now galvanised scenes of collective emotion such as they had previously known from Rossini's *Mosè*, *Maometto II*, and *Semiramide* or Bellini's *Norma*. Right at the start, the chorus of exiled Jews (visibly and audibly arrayed as levites, maidens, and the collectivity) gives voice to alternate moods of sorrow, entreaty, and defiance; the clear structure pares down the expansive musical development found in Rossini. Throughout the opera, Verdi ruthlessly shrinks recitative, brings on events at startling pace, and takes short cuts through the conventional forms of Italian opera.

Those forms – codified by Rossini – built an opera out of large-scale units in which the dominant feeling moved as a rule from meditation to action, the music, often, from slow to fast. An aria generally contained, after a passage of recitative to establish the situation and the mood, a meditative first section ('cantabile'); a bridge passage would set off – perhaps through the arrival of a piece of news or the character's own altered stance – a discharge of feeling expressed in an often faster closing section known as a 'cabaletta'. Duets, larger concerted passages, and first-act finales involving the whole cast and the chorus were likewise built in sections: Rossini's famous duets in *Semiramide* had three basic sections (fast–slow–fast) with, in the middle, an opportunity for melting, melismatic vocal display by the two voices together; musical structure prevailed over dramatic conflict, for in Rossini (and at times in Bellini and Donizetti) the voices might utter conflicting sentiments to the same music.

Before Verdi's breakthrough Mercadante had set out a programme for making these elementary forms more dramatic by at once varying and simplifying them – by, for instance, dropping 'trivial' cabalettas, band music, needless coloratura display, and the arbitrary Rossinian crescendo. It was Verdi who successfully carried out the programme – not all at once. He was also the first consistently to let into Italian music the full blast of high Romantic feeling.

Italian audiences, steeped in the classics with their urge to decorum and proportion, had withstood the onset of Romanticism and especially the new cult of the extreme, the remote, and the bizarre. Bellini, after two early ventures into Romantic frenzy in *Il pirata* and *La straniera*, had deliberately moved towards a more poised simplicity. Verdi alone put across in opera the verbal lightning flashes and earthquakes deployed by the most influential literature of the decade and a half up to the failed revolutions of 1848. Such books as, in English, Carlyle's *Past and Present* (1843), in French Lamennais's *A Believer Speaks* (1834), in Italian Gioberti's *Of the Civil and Moral Primacy of the Italians*

(1843) – high-pitched, repetitive, hortatory – are now to varying degrees unreadable. In their own time they were hugely successful; they voiced the high aspirations that were to come crashing in 1848.

Behind such works stood the German Romantic literature of a generation earlier. Verdi did not read German, but in 1845 he significantly directed Piave to Mme de Staël's *On Germany*, which had introduced that literature to Latin Europe. He admired – in translation – not only Schiller's vast dramas but Werner's equally vast, gloomy tragedy *Attila*: the subject was 'extremely fine, grand, and most effective', the choruses 'stupendous', the libretto, once Solera had written it for him, 'fine, excellent for setting to music' (BM, 143–4, 154–5, 158; C, 132, 138). This is the libretto in which the Huns' chorus sings 'Tonight we feast on wine, tomorrow on severed heads and limbs'; when Covent Garden put on the work in 1990 the producer, Elijah Moshinsky, cut roughly a third of it out of the surtitles, no doubt on the well-taken consideration that it would have brought guffaws. Yet Verdi relished it, as he did Byron's heroics and Hugo's rodomontade and extravagant theatrical coups: he shared wholeheartedly the taste of his own day.

Solera, from 1841 to 1846 the librettist of *Nabucco*, *Lombardi*, *Giovanna d'Arco*, and *Attila*, later struck Verdi as having been potentially 'the leading author of opera librettos of our time' (BM, 162). That was not till 1861, when Solera – a rolling-stone adventurer – had left opera behind; at the time Verdi, it seems, left out the 'potentially', for until the last of these four operas he set the words pretty well without question. Solera thought big, organised grand set pieces, understood musical forms – and let Verdi in not only for the carnivorous Huns but for the devils' waltz-time chorus in *Giovanna d'Arco* ('Tu sei bella'), which now seems one of the feebler things in the early works. At the time it was the hit of the show, endlessly resounding from barrel organs.

What Verdi made of these texts is another matter. The Huns' chorus goes by so fast that not one word is audible; the music drives in an urgent sense of wildness, and that is enough. The devils' chorus perpetrates, at worst, 'innocent vulgarity'.[5] At this stage in Verdi's career an essay in delicate orchestral writing like I due Foscari (1844) could not avoid the monotony due to a weepy libretto: speed and energy were his strong suit; his insistence on them cut out a great deal of flummery. In Nabucco, rather than the great choruses (whose real impact, as we shall see, came later), what struck the original audience was the vocal drama of the two main parts, expressed in musical structures more closely wedded to the action than had been the rule.

The unbiblical part of Abigaille encompasses delicate coloratura and extraordinarily vehement, spiky vocal writing to bring out the conflict within the character – Nebuchadnezzar's illegitimate child by a slave woman, torn between love for a Jew and overreaching ambition. The swoops and peaks in the recitative that opens Act 2, and the repeated outcries and downward runs in the cabaletta 'Salgo già del trono aurato' as she imagines kings' daughters begging at the feet of the 'humble slave' – these derive from Bellini's Norma; but where Norma's passion kept a measure of classical dignity, Abigaille is nearly all vocal push and go, and accordingly hard to cast. (Both parts are notoriously difficult. Norma, however, with the right actress-singer brings great rewards; Abigaille can seem wearing.)

Nabucco himself gave Verdi the chance to write for Giorgio Ronconi a baritone part of the kind familiar from many of his later operas – high-lying, merciless in its call on great resources of firm legato singing, yet allowing for dramatic interruptions in the flow, like the king's lapse into depressed, almost incoherent utterance when, in the Act 2 finale, God's lightning strikes the crown from his blasphemous head. Ronconi had done something like it in Donizetti's Torquato Tasso and other works, Bellini too had written baritone arias on a line at once mellifluous and pressing, but from then on people would speak of 'Verdi baritone' parts. They would often complain that keeping the voice in such a high tessitura strained and ruined it. Verdi, however, wrote for baritones like Ronconi and Felice Varesi who could exploit their high register for high drama; the appeal of such parts later brought forward more singers who could manage them, while wrecking others who could not.

For the solo writing in these parts there were precedents. The Act 3 duet, however, was something new. Abigaille makes the captive Nabucco seal the fate of the Jews, among them his legitimate daughter, a convert. Through all the changes of situation and mood either character's vocal line cleaves to what she or he feels: Abigaille's jaunty imperiousness at the start, her exuberance (cue for vocal fireworks) as she tears up the evidence of her birth, her bright soaring contemplation of her own greatness, Nabucco's shame, his abject plea for forgiveness – these individual, varied sections are all dovetailed to intensely dramatic effect. From then on, critics might complain for years of vulgarity and noise, Delacroix – an out-and-out Romantic in his own art but a musical conservative – might pun on 'Verdi or Merdi';[6] the audience had experienced an operatic conflict more sharply etched than anything it had known; it did not look back.

Solera's love of grandiose scenes, with principals and chorus in pseudo-historical confrontation, appears to have satisfied Verdi through *Lombardi* and *Giovanna d'Arco* – works more ramshackle than *Nabucco*, though each had sublime moments like the trio of baptism in *Lombardi* to balance others when mechanical ostinato accompaniments or blatant brass doubling of the voice parts took over.

After *Giovanna*, Verdi began to move away from Solera. His experience over the work made him vow no longer to have anything to do with La Scala or with its impresario Merelli, a vow he kept for over twenty years: engagements outside Milan implied less reliance on the Milan-based Solera, though Verdi still sought him out for *Attila*. Once into composing it he came to feel in the libretto a want of novelty – for him, a constant requirement. It did fire his inspiration with at least one great choral scene – the Pope miraculously compels Attila to lift the siege of Rome – but as rehearsals drew near Verdi no longer wished to end it on yet another such tableau; he chose to focus the denouement on the principals alone. Solera, by then abroad, did not

6 Verdi's chief librettist Francesco Maria Piave, with whom he collaborated from 1843 to 1862. Portrait by G. Favretto

answer in time his urgent request for new matter; Verdi therefore called on Piave, with whom he had already worked on *Ernani* and *I due Foscari*.

According to an influential comment, Verdi's meeting with Piave in 1843 was his 'first opportunity to work with himself': through the young Venetian, 'scarcely more than an instrument in his hands', he could project his own ideas, often his own words.[7] Not that Verdi acknowledged this, save by going back to Piave again and again. At conscious level he had greater esteem for two poets apparently more distinguished – Andrea Maffei, who wrote him the awkward libretto of *I masnadieri* (1847), and the Naples-based Salvadore Cammarano, an experienced man who collaborated with him on four operas, from *Alzira* (1845) to *Il trovatore* (1853). To Cammarano he was at first deferential: he excused himself twice for asking whether three arias in a row were not too many (C, 430); though he later had to struggle against the librettist's custom-bound view of dramatic propriety, he still put forward suggestions rather than demands and the two men dealt on equal terms.

With the inexperienced Piave Verdi could be at once didactic and rough; though Piave learnt a good deal Verdi went on being rough. After they had worked together on six operas he could still ditch a whole libretto Piave had written specially for him because a better idea had just struck him (it turned into *La traviata*). In his letters mock insults ('swine', 'cat', 'crocodile', 'rat') and mock threats to curse or murder Piave alternated with crumbs of comfort: 'be fond of me, because to tell the truth, though it doesn't look like it, I am a little bit fond of you' (BM, 150, 152).

Ernani (1844), their first collaboration, had likewise meant ditching Piave's first offering. Hugo's play, a riotous scandal on its first Paris appearance in 1830, attracted Verdi by the very extravagance of its premise – the 'point of honour' that leads the hero to kill himself on his wedding night because his worst enemy has made him swear to do so on the blowing of the horn. He urged on Piave brevity, action, 'fire'; each act ought to be shorter than the previous one. When he got the libretto he complained that the recitatives were too long; if *Ernani* was to interrupt the desperate last-act trio with a solo what were the other two characters to do? Yet his further complaint that the libretto thrust on the prima donna an unmanageable sequence of a big aria, a duet turning into a trio, and a finale one after the other did not stop him from burdening Sofia Loewe with just that (BM, 53–4, 65, 71, 91–2, 102). In their joint ventures two and three years later he would still urge on Piave 'Passion! Passion! Never mind which, but passion!'; he wanted 'poetry with great big balls'.[8]

Ernani has been described as 'a youthful, passionate female voice [. . .] besieged by three male voices, each of whom establishes a special relationship with her'; none, not even the tenor, achieves full union, and the conflict is resolved by a wind instrument, the horn.[9] This has the merit of bringing out the pre-eminence in the work, not of 'characters' but of individual voices deployed in emotional contest. Shaw put it another way: Ernani was 'that ultra-classical product of romanticism, the grandiose Italian opera in which the executive art consists in a splendid display of personal heroics, and the drama arises out of the simplest and most universal stimulants to them'.[10]

Even more than Nabucco, Ernani launched Verdi's European fame; it headed a line of works that dropped Solera's part awesome, part grotesque collective tableaux in favour of what John Donne called a negotiation of souls; it remained one of the Verdian staples through the individualistic nineteenth century, even when the other early operas had fallen out of use. Today it is seldom given, no doubt because a soprano, tenor, and baritone able to do it justice are hard to find and, when they turn up, the management would rather have them sing Il trovatore, a work similar in feeling. Yet a committed performance by artists who are not yet or never will be stars can rouse headlong delight: one such, at St Pancras (now Camden) Town Hall in 1963, conducted by Franz Manton with Pauline Tinsley as Elvira, still resounds in memory.

In Elvira's double aria near the start, the waltz-time cantabile ('Ernani, Ernani involami') takes off in an extraordinary surge near the end of the stanza: the voice gradually opens a huge window onto a night-blue sky. Verdi was to work more such effects at crucial moments; Bellini and Donizetti had done something like it, but he did it more consistently and rapidly – by an unexpected modulation, or by extending the melodic line into higher notes and wider intervals, or into a new phrase such as the noble, exclamatory one ('e vincitor de' secoli') that forms the climax of Charles V's Act 3 meditation 'Oh de' verd'anni miei'.

Charles is, still more than Nabucco, the original 'Verdi baritone', using his upper register and command of legato to work effects from the seductive to the monumentally heroic. The nobility of line he achieves in Act 3, not only at the place just noted but in the impressive arioso that precedes it and in his address to the spirit of Charlemagne, 'O sommo Carlo', makes it seem natural that the conspirators who were about to murder him should, as he chooses forgiveness, join and acclaim him; with him they end the act in a wave-like ensemble at once driving and grand. Noble eloquence was to be a mark of Verdi's writing – in baritone and bass parts especially – an attribute shared with Gluck, Beethoven, Elgar, not many more.

The characteristic of *Ernani* everyone notices is dynamism. In one or two choruses this begs for Gilbert and Sullivan parody ('With catlike tread'). Elsewhere the sheer drive exhilarates. It is far from uncalculated: for the sake of moving on Verdi deliberately shortened and made asymmetrical what he had first drafted as a symmetrical sixteen-bar passage. 'As though launched from a catapult'[11] could describe not just Elvira's and Ernani's defiance at the trio climax to her and Charles's duet of conflict but many other passages. Yet something that begins in huge urgency and ends in breakneck self-sacrifice like the Elvira–Ernani duet in Act 2 (again turning into a trio, this time with the doom-bearing bass) slows and softens along the way into a moment of reconciliation ('Non son rea') with, at Ernani's blurting out that he still loves her, a pre-echo of the best-known passionate outburst in the whole of Verdi's work, 'Amami, Alfredo' from *La traviata*. A yet nearer foretaste is the three measures in alternate major minor just ahead of the final trio (they replaced a duettino which Verdi cut): a 'sublime lyrical outpouring in octaves, a musical apotheosis of the passion of Elvira and Ernani [. . .] the first musical gesture in Verdi that so succinctly yet completely summarises a complex web of emotions'.[12]

Ernani indeed told of many things to come in the Verdi works now universally familiar, less in its instrumental writing – often poster-like, in spite of good things such as the oboe that shadows Ernani himself in the final trio and the bass clarinet that comes in as he dies – than in the vocal casting and the treatment of the voice itself.

By Verdi's time the vocal casting of opera was changing. The robust, passionate tenor was coming in, though he was still expected to show lyric clarity of voice. He now sang the lover's part – not the tenor's assignment in the eighteenth century, and not always in Rossini; as the lover he must sound virile. In Verdi's operas he would not, as in Bellini's, sing in his head voice extraordinary notes like high F. A dying convention gave the lover's part to a female contralto in breeches, but Verdi would have none of it. True, in his eagerness to have the controversial plot of *Ernani* approved in Venice he at first accepted such casting – perhaps with a mental reservation; he shortly demanded and got a tenor. Along with the 'Verdi baritone' he brought forward the stern unyielding bass, usually as a father figure. For none of his male parts was he to write coloratura as his predecessors had.

Abigaille had made fiercer still the existing dramatic soprano, but those later heroines whose character was strong and their vocal line spiky – the freedom fighter Odabella in *Attila*, Lady Macbeth – fell short of her overwrought excess. Following on from *Ernani*, the mark of most Verdi heroines was to be, in Shaw's words, 'tragic beauty', that of most Verdi men 'superb distinction and heroic force'.[13] Coloratura writing in leading women's parts, from Abigaille down to *La traviata* (1853), as a rule sought to bring out character and situation rather than to adorn. Verdi took further a trend already evident in Bellini and Donizetti, where coloratura is seldom the canary display early twentieth-century audiences took it for. Elvira's cantabile near the start of *Ernani* outdoes its Donizettian equivalents in compactness and drive; coloratura runs tell us that she is high-souled and rare as well as beautiful; staccato glitter in the cabaletta ('Tutto sprezzo che d'Ernani') tells of her pride and dash.

In the singers of nearly all his leading parts Verdi looked for 'spark', 'spirit', 'passion', 'having the devil in [them]' (C, 390, 612; IEV, 319–20). He often stressed ability to act and to bring out the words, if need be at the expense of vocal beauty. This should be taken with a pinch of salt, especially in his early phase. Italian audiences of the 1830s and 1840s made a cult of the voice, far more than did German or French; the young German composer Otto Nicolai was bowled over, on his arrival in Italy in 1833, by the quality of voice the now forgotten Almerinda Manzocchi showed and by her virtuoso skill in its use. A good many singers excelled in these but were duff actors. That explains something like Verdi's famous letter to Cammarano of 1848, arguing that Eugenia Tadolini was too highly qualified to sing Lady Macbeth (or, as he often called her, 'Lady') when the opera, already given in Florence with another singer, reached Naples:

> Tadolini is a fine figure of a woman, and I should like Lady Macbeth to look ugly and evil. Tadolini sings to perfection; and I would rather that Lady didn't sing at all. Tadolini has a wonderful voice, clear, limpid, and strong; and I would rather that Lady's voice were rough, hollow, stifled. Tadolini's voice has something angelic in it. Lady's should have something devilish. (C, 61–2)

Tadolini, a virtuoso singer but not much of an actress, was clearly meant to be shown the letter and jolted into greater expressiveness: 'to combat the narcissistic disposition of the Italian prima donna a touch of exaggeration was needed'.[14] Vocal beauty was not something Verdi could disregard, least of all in the early works; it glorifies them, as Joan Sutherland showed in her famous recording of 'Ernani, Ernani involami'. His demand for acting ability sharpened in the latter half of the century, when all the arts, opera included, moved closer to realism. Yet when, in 1877, he commended Adelina Patti as a 'great actress', her acting ability in perfect balance with her singing (C, 624–5), he scarcely had in mind – other accounts of her suggest – an operatic Mrs Siddons: much of Patti's 'great acting' was musicianly control of a peerless voice. Five years earlier Verdi had laid down a general rule: 'in opera what is needed above all is musicality: fire, spirit, vigour, and enthusiasm'.[15]

In the 1840s, a young singer like Erminia Frezzolini, who created the leading women characters in Lombardi and Giovanna d'Arco and went on to sing many Verdian parts, united the skill and intensity these called for. So did the original Ernani and Elvira, Carlo Guasco and Sofia Loewe, though on the opening night Guasco (virtually frog-marched into the part at short notice after Verdi had rejected two other potential tenors) was perilously hoarse and Loewe out of tune. As sometimes happened, the work was a success anyhow; later performances recovered and speeded it on its lightning career. Within six months some twenty Italian theatres gave it, as did Vienna and, in the following year, London, Lisbon, and Madrid.

After the triple success of Nabucco, Lombardi, and Ernani (1842–4) Verdi could make contracts with impresarios for new operas, and with publishers for the rights in the score and the printing rights, on terms not yet such as to break all Italian records, but better than were open to his contemporaries.

The publisher of music derived from opera had come on the Italian scene in the early 1800s; until then the hand copyist had ruled. By the 1840s the publisher had grown in importance. A composer whose new opera succeeded in one theatre could profit, first by selling him the whole or a share in the manuscript score and parts, to be copied by hand and hired out to other theatres; and then by selling the right to print the vocal score as well as single numbers arranged for all kinds of solo voices and instruments.

The rights in the score were as yet a doubtful proposition: for lack of enforceable copyright, managements could easily buy a stolen copy or get a routine composer to work up an orchestral accompaniment from the printed vocal score. Through such piracy Bellini had lost all potential Italian earnings from his enormously successful Paris opera I puritani. Printed arrangements, however, were a reliable money-maker so long as publisher and composer got them out right on top of a successful first performance, before pirates could strike: in an age when the upper classes were opera-mad and modern recording and broadcasting media unknown, only transcriptions let people enjoy the latest hit number in their own drawing-room.

From the start of his career Verdi dealt with two of the leading Milan publishers, Ricordi and Lucca. With four generations of the Ricordi family he was to have a lifelong relationship, marked by occasional storms but profitable to both; Verdi became the publisher's mainstay.

Giovanni Ricordi, the founder, was still largely a printer and seller of sheet music. In the ten years after the first production of *Lombardi* he published the opera or numbers from it in no fewer than 245 arrangements – for solo cornet, for soprano and tenor in the key of G throughout, and so on: more than the firm ever made from any other work. This was good for Ricordi, less so for Verdi, who had sold the rights for a flat fee. Only after *Macbeth* would he be able to work out with Ricordi a means of steadily exploiting his operas in theatres over much of the world.

With Francesco Lucca, once a breakaway Ricordi apprentice, Verdi's relationship was sour from the start. An action Lucca brought against Ricordi over the rights in the words of *Nabucco* held up for some months productions of the opera away from La Scala: this at the very moment of the composer's breakthrough. Verdi none the less had to go on doing business with Lucca, to whom he had originally sold a half-share in the music. Lucca badgered him for more, bought from a third party the publishing rights in the future *Attila*, and at length got Verdi to sign two contracts for what became *I masnadieri* and *Il corsaro*; by an innovatory step, Lucca bought up all the rights and was to arrange the production and casting.

He then spoilt his own game: he insisted that Verdi should write the operas at times that did not suit him, *Masnadieri* (put off from 1846 by Verdi's breakdown in health) for London in July 1847, and then, when London had after all struck the composer as a vein of gold he might at once return to, *Corsaro* for Trieste in 1848 – and he did so in a manner that struck Verdi as inflexible and harsh; by the time of *Corsaro* he had become 'this exceedingly greedy and tactless Signor Lucca' (*C*, 461). Verdi threw off *Corsaro* as a potboiler and let it be put on in his absence, though he did send the prima donna cogent advice; he then wiped his hands of Lucca.

The equivalent villain among impresarios was Merelli. Verdi had strong reasons for deciding in 1845 to have no more to do with him or, since he was a fixture there, with La Scala. Though Merelli had launched him as a composer, and had probably helped him over his dejection at the loss of Margherita, the 'Napoleon of impresarios' was essentially a theatrical agent on a large scale, too busy and vainglorious to look after the detail of productions; the resulting slovenliness put off Donizetti as well.

The right impresario for Verdi at a crucial point in his early career was Alessandro Lanari. Unlike Merelli, he was above all an organiser of scenery, costumes, and crowds, in effect a producer at a time when no such figure was ever billed. He could also be mean and unpleasant; he had to be if he was to keep afloat his management of multiple opera seasons, a large costume workshop, and a theatrical agency in a poor country that paid far less for opera than could London, Paris, and Madrid. He and Verdi first came together over *Attila*, which Lanari put on in Venice. A few months later they contracted for an opera to be given early in 1847 at Lanari's home theatre, La Pergola in the cultivated city of Florence. This – Verdi was clear – would be an important work; Lanari was to pay him 18,000 francs, easily a record fee for an Italian opera. It would be his masterpiece, in the old sense of the work that entitled a craftsman to master's rank. He would take advantage of impresario and city to write an opera based on an exalted literary source; in the end the text he chose was *Macbeth*.

Verdi was among Shakespeare's first Italian admirers. A full translation of the plays appeared as late as 1838; the first reasonably faithful performance of one of them (*Othello*) was hissed off the Milan stage in 1842. Italy was thus half a generation behind France, and half a century behind Germany, in coming to terms with a dramatist

7 The smoking ruins of Aquileia: sketch for the first scene of Attila (Venice, La Fenice, 1846) by the stage designer Giuseppe Bertoja

previously thought uncouth, who wrote in a language few continentals could read. Verdi, from the start a reader of the 1838 translation, never doubted that Shakespeare outdid his other major literary sources, Schiller and Hugo, above all in the way he 'analyse[d] the human mind so acutely and penetrate[d] it so profoundly', 'that grandeur, that breadth, that sublime, rarefied, and strange atmosphere' (IEV, 218, 341; VR 82–85, 88). He never learnt to spell Shakespeare's name (nor did Shakespeare); yet the plays furnished his mind.

As early as 1843 *King Lear* was one of the works Verdi thought of as a possible basis for his Venice opera (ultimately *Ernani*); it would haunt him for the next decade and a half. As he later glanced at *Hamlet* and composed *Othello* Verdi clearly saw the challenge Shakespeare set him in the four major tragedies. For *Macbeth* he made sure not only of Lanari's skills but of a high baritone who could act, Felice Varesi.

'This tragedy', Verdi wrote to his chosen librettist Piave, 'is one of the greatest of human creations! . . . If we can't make something great out of it let's at least try to make something uncommon' (A, I, 643). As Francesco Degrada has argued in a penetrating essay, Verdi set about achieving this in two ways: first he cut down the tragedy to 'a bare, lucid, pitiless psychological diagram', and secondly he used music, space, scenery, and costumes to create a complex theatrical spectacle on more than one plane – an unsystematic forerunner of Wagner's music drama uniting the resources of all the arts.[16]

'Brevity and sublimity', Verdi had as usual directed Piave. The librettist, however, botched the job. His text, Verdi thundered – partly in capitals – was banal and, worse still, prolix: 'FEW WORDS . . . FEW WORDS . . . FEW, FEW BUT SIGNIFICANT' (A, I, 644–5). He got Maffei to rewrite the witches' parts and the sleepwalking scene but threw out some of his contributions too; in the end the printed libretto was anonymous. Some of it Verdi himself had dictated; for the plotting of Banquo's murder (with Lady Macbeth more active than in Shakespeare) he insisted on a kind of shorthand exchange: 'A fresh crime?' 'It has to be!' He cut out Lady Macduff and her son, most of the minor characters, all the English scenes but for Macduff's agony at the slaughter of his wife and children (framed by an exiles' chorus), and reduced Duncan to a walk-on. There were, he later wrote, three parts in the opera, Macbeth, Lady Macbeth, and the witches (made into a chorus): only a slight exaggeration, for the two tenors (Macduff and Malcolm) have little enough, while Banquo's short, noble bass part ends halfway through.

In cutting through to his 'psychological diagram' – Degrada argues – Verdi was hampered by Italian blindness to the supernatural as anything other than angels and devils, incomers familiar from Roman Catholic imagery. *Macbeth* was seen – and, by its original audience, misunderstood – as belonging to the 'fantastic' genre, like Meyerbeer's *Robert le Diable* with its balletic nuns' ghosts. Verdi, helped by his reading of the German critic A. W. Schlegel, got part way to a 'Protestant' understanding of the witches as inner demons, but could not quite shake off Italian convention: the witches' music is at times apt, elsewhere tinny.

For *Macbeth* as a spectacle on many levels Verdi could draw on the resources of the mid nineteenth-century theatre. They may now seem tawdry to those used to special computer effects in the cinema; they could seem wonderful to contemporaries like Baudelaire:

> I have now and then seen
> At one end of a commonplace theatre
> Set ablaze by a resounding orchestra
> A fairy light up in a hellish sky
> A miraculous dawn;
> I have now and then seen at one end of a commonplace theatre
> A being who was nothing but light, gold, and gauze
> Bring huge Satan crashing [...] ('L'irréparable')

As he set about achieving like effects Verdi knew what to avoid. In leading Italian opera houses, management contracts laid down that principals' costumes must be made wholly of silk and velvet: he insisted on coarser, medieval-looking stuff. The Banquo wished to exercise a soloist's privilege of not walking on as ghost: Verdi overrode him. What he specially wanted to bring off was the apparitions scene, with a 'phantasmagoria' – the nightmare vision of Banquo's descendants – not unlike Baudelaire's conjuring trick with gauze and light, accompanied by eerie music literally, as in some Shakespearean stage directions, underground. The visual device, it seems, did not work as Verdi had hoped, but the sound from a group of two oboes, six clarinets, two bassoons, and one contrabassoon floated up from its trapdoor – he later recalled – 'strange, mysterious, and at the same time calm and subdued' (C, 453). It was 'one of the most unearthly sounds in nineteenth-century opera, all the more disconcerting for the simplicity of the music itself'.[17]

We do not now hear this sound exactly as Verdi wrote it in 1847, because in 1865 he adapted *Macbeth* for Paris and the new version has stuck – in many ways finer, yet, with Verdi's style in the new passages much evolved, something of a patchwork. A good deal remains that justifies our calling even the 1847 version a work of genius, above all the sleepwalking scene, unchanged in 1865. The tune to which Lady Macbeth creeps onstage and whose 'infinite sense of oppression and exhaustion'[18] comes back yet never seems to repeat, the quick 'handwashing' arpeggio on muted strings, the chromatic upward scale that dogs the sleepwalker like a quiet fate, the other instrumental comments falling delicate on the morbid hush, the orchestral chords that take the wandering mind through remote keys – these are at once original (Italian opera had nothing like them), simple, and utterly right.

The other high spot – along with the apparitions scene – was a good deal revised in 1865: the duet in which Lady Macbeth nerves her husband to kill Duncan. Here and in the sleepwalking scene Verdi took great pains with the original singers, Varesi and Marianna Barbieri-Nini. He enjoined 'sotto voce', 'hollow tone', singing 'with mutes on'; he drove in the 'significant words'; he imposed what felt like endless rehearsals.

The needs of opera distil the great speeches in the original down to a few essential words, but the music finds equivalents for 'heaven's cherubim hors'd' and 'the multitudinous seas incarnadine' in brief, eloquent lyrical outbursts; it recreates the moment-to-moment rush of feeling in Shakespeare through lithe and responsive melodic invention and, in the orchestra, subtle writing for winds, timpani, and muted strings; it makes concise, triumphant use of Italian operatic form when Lady Macbeth, taunting, morally blind, repeats in sunny major the tune her husband has just despairingly uttered in the minor, and again (though here the reviser's hand has been at work) in the breathless stretta to which the couple go off on the knocking at the gate. It is all highly articulated and dynamic, still more than the remarkable duets of conflict and contrast in previous operas. Those who know the music of this and the sleepwalking scene may find that it invades their inner ear when they next witness the original play.

If all of *Macbeth* were on that level it would be incomparable. Much in it is fine – the initial duet in which Macbeth and Banquo pithily counter one another's view of the witches, the rolling, relentless Act 1 finale after the discovery of the murder, Lady Macbeth's aria 'La luce langue', the exiles' chorus – the last two written or rewritten in 1865 style, subtle and flexible so as to stand out a trifle incongruously from the rest. Lady Macbeth's 1847 solos run to vocal peaks and troughs, Abigaille-like but better controlled; her toast in the banquet scene puts a bold, shrill face on her unease: just right. So too the tinny little march as the village band plays Duncan into the castle has an innocence that throws into relief the impending murder. Other passages, not just for the witches, share some of the crudities of Verdi's early style; in neither version is the ending quite apt. Yet modern Italian critics have at times seen *Macbeth* as Verdi's finest Shakespearean work, because in composing it he did not illustrate a revered classic but – firmly, lucidly, with the whole 'granite-like integrity of his moral world' engaged – took on a powerful drama and recreated it wholesale as opera.[19]

With *Macbeth* behind him, Verdi could go on to outdo all other composers in his field. This meant working outside Italy, perhaps in London, certainly in Paris. His Paris venture was to bring him together with the woman who from then on shared his life.

8 Verdi in his late thirties

3 Turning-points, 1847–1849: *I masnadieri* to *La battaglia di Legnano*; Strepponi, revolution and Sant'Agata

After *Macbeth* Verdi had new fields to conquer. To begin with they were abroad. Italian opera composers had long pursued in foreign capitals the sort of money they could never earn at home.

The most glittering precedent was Rossini. In Paris he had made himself for a time the ruling deity of both French and Italian opera; Bellini and Donizetti had followed. In Verdi's lifetime the city was the European capital of intellect, journalism, and fashion; success there conferred prestige as well as money. By 1845, a few years into his career, invitations began to come his way. He was entering his worst period of overwork: though tied up for the next two years, he looked for a short cut – a libretto he could use both to fulfil a contract in Italy and, slightly adapted, to win the highest prize, the Paris Opéra with its exclusive diet of elaborate works sung in French. Only on his first trip abroad – in June 1847 it took him briefly to Paris on the way to London – did he commit himself; even then he would make his début with an adaptation of an existing Italian work, *I lombardi*.[1]

Before leaving in late May, Verdi had begun to negotiate another important contract, this time with his Italian publisher Ricordi for a future opera (ultimately *La battaglia di Legnano*, 1849). It signalled a new departure that would enhance his earnings, cut down his work rate, and, at long last, free him from the galleys. The outcome was fully clear only in the mid 1850s. Meanwhile Verdi and his faithful assistant Muzio took in the Swiss Alps, a journey by water down the

Rhine, castle-gazing, then by the new railway from Cologne to Brussels and Paris, finally by sea to Dover and London.

What Verdi made of his travels we scarcely know. London, when he got there early in June, struck him as the greatest city in the world, extraordinary in its wealth and imperial splendour. The weather, alas, was bad, the smoke from thousands of chimneys overpowering, the food heavy, the language incomprehensible. But for sorties to the theatre and to one five-hour dinner Verdi kept his head down, working on the opera he had come to launch, I masnadieri, and seeing almost no one.

Masnadieri, written for the star singer of the day, Jenny Lind, has been called 'Verdi's worst opera', too long, too self-conscious, with few memorable numbers and a general lack of his 'angry glimpses' and 'sublime condensations'.[2] Work on it probably suffered from Verdi's having had to break off for Macbeth, and then, after that mighty effort, from his creative exhaustion. Maffei's libretto made heavy going of Schiller's 'storm and stress' drama, Verdi fumbled the evil brother's crucial soliloquy, and Lind's old-fashioned, highly ornamented vocalism dictated some tinselly music. Acclamation on the first night led only to scant success in later performances.

Verdi had made almost no contact with London away from the opera, but for visits to Shakespeare performances. He liked the countryside and the gentlemanly manner of the opera impresario Benjamin Lumley; for a while he contemplated a possible run of London seasons (April to August), with a lavish contract to write an opera a year and conduct others and a leafy cottage to escape to. Nothing came of this; talk of it may not have been seriously meant. When in Italy, Verdi sometimes pointed to the golden opportunities he was missing in London and Paris – he mentioned, about this time, fancy figures like 80,000 or even 100,000 francs for an opera; Masnadieri had brought him in 20,000 – just as in Paris he later bemoaned the loss of openings in Italy that would have earned him more money.

This was in part the haggling common in the opera world, but it had a real basis. Paris especially could bring in a lot of money – after a composer had invested much time in preparation and more in waiting: a French opera generally earned, not a flat fee as in Italy, but a royalty on each performance; if it succeeded it would go on doing so for many years, and in many theatres away from Paris. Italy meant a lower fee but only a short, sharp effort, and it paid at once. There were times when one or the other seemed preferable.

Verdi soon experienced what writing a Paris grand opera meant. *Jérusalem*, the work he and his French librettists adapted from *Lombardi*, with the music extensively revised and a compulsory ballet, took the stage less than five months after his arrival. That was fast going for a house where his two later grand operas demanded rehearsal periods of about nine and seven months apiece (each time with a break of three or four weeks) and composition took longer still; true, each was a newly-coined work and ran to the full Paris length of five acts.

Such timetables flowed from the merits of the Opéra as well as from its defects. Verdi had no doubt of the merits: the production of *Jérusalem* would be 'absolutely magnificent' (C, 464). Since the huge success of Meyerbeer's *Robert le Diable* (1831) the house had specialised in blockbusters on themes that allowed both an edifying history lesson and plenty of thrills, even some titillation along the way, the whole enacted by masses of singers, dancers, and extras against grandiose, historically accurate sets. Together with bureaucratic management, all this made for what Strepponi later called the Opéra's 'machinery of marble and lead'; it took, she said, twenty-four hours to decide whether a singer should raise a finger or the whole hand (WalkerV, 267).

The defects were musical. 'I have never heard worse singers', Verdi declared soon after his arrival, 'or a more mediocre chorus.' Even the orchestra was 'little better than middling' – this in Paris, together with Germany the fount of orchestral music (A, I, 711). Verdi never went back on his first impression, though he later praised one or two singers. The basic trouble was too many cooks: each of a number of officials demanded this and that in the name of exclusive Parisian 'good taste'. 'Manufacture' did duty for inspiration; 'you end up not with an opera written all at one go but with a *mosaic*' (C, 220–1). Yet, notwithstanding his caustic view of the 'big shop', Verdi negotiated for Paris contracts year after year.

The reason was in part money. In part, too, Verdi needed to challenge on his own ground a composer whose European fame, based on his Paris grand operas, is now hard to credit: from about 1840 to 1880 Meyerbeer seemed to the cognoscenti much the profounder artist, a thinker and 'scientific' musician as Verdi would never be. Finally, Paris delivered not just fame but the pleasure of everyday living: Verdi liked it.

Besides stays of about two years each in 1847–49 and 1853–55 and a year in 1866–67, all partly taken up with a new French opera, Verdi was in Paris – on average for two months or so at a time – in 1852, 1856–57, 1862–63 (four times), 1870, 1873, 1875, 1876, 1880, 1882, 1886, and 1894 (twice) – far more often than he went to the capital of united Italy. On some of these visits too he was concerned with putting on an opera – an existing one in a French or an adapted version – on others he was looking after his investments, but much of the time he enjoyed the great city and, above all, its theatres of all kinds.

Right at the start he appreciated the 'free life' he could lead in Paris: he need visit or be visited by no one, no one pointed him out as people did in Italian towns (A, 1, 711, 735). His fame ran there as elsewhere, but Paris was so big and so full of celebrated artists that in practice he could be anonymous. More generally, Paris offered freedom of speech and of the press undreamt of in Italy, in a language Verdi soon felt at home with; he became a keen newspaper reader and, in later years in Italy, read the Paris *Figaro*. On his first visits he stayed in a rented flat, later in hotels, always within easy reach of the theatre district along the boulevards of the right bank; the hotels got grander with time, until at length he reached the Grand Hotel, across from the new Opéra (now the Opéra-Garnier). He took occasional summer breaks in an outer suburb or, later, in the Pyrenees; in Paris he appears to have socialised little outside the theatre, where opera was no more than the chief ornament.

Paris had long been the capital of European theatre, not just of drama with literary pretensions such as Victor Hugo's but of show business. Its plays and vaudevilles, often turned out by partnerships of authors, went all over Europe and the Americas and fed the librettos of Italian opera. When he could, Verdi went to the theatre night after night. During his long stay in 1847–49 he probably took in at first hand the plays he would soon use as the bases of *Luisa Miller* and *Stiffelio*; he also picked up ideas about production, like multiple scenery that showed action on different levels, or simultaneously inside and outside a house, which he was to exploit in the last scenes of *Aida* and *Rigoletto*.[3]

The Parisian spoken theatre made far greater use of music than we might think, particularly of *mélodrame* (music played under speech); this might punctuate a drama in as many as seventy places, above all in '*scènes mystérieuses*'. Verdi was not above appropriating such means: the dénouement in *Stiffelio*, when the minister forgives his errant wife in front of the congregation, follows the musical plan of the Paris *mélodrame* in that scene.[4]

Verdi's first long stay in Paris confirmed the artistic maturity he had just reached in *Macbeth*; the two experiences together let him grasp the full possibilities of theatre as the mid nineteenth century cultivated them. In his intimate life Paris meant a profound change: he and Giuseppina Strepponi met again there; they became lovers, decided to live together, and did so for the next half-century.

Already at the time of *Nabucco* in 1842, Strepponi – then twenty-six – had behind her a tumultuous career. She was two years younger than Verdi and, like him, a Lombard in the broad sense then current, though from the opposite side of the river Po; they shared both musical taste and political outlook. The daughter of a composer, herself a trained musician, Strepponi had early become the family breadwinner; as a soprano able to compass both the tragic and the gentler heroines of Bellini and Donizetti she won great, almost immediate success. Life as head of a family, independent woman, and opera star put her under great pressure; in the outcome she mismanaged both her career and her personal life.

By the first performance of *Nabucco* her voice was in ruins. A year's rest helped somewhat: in spring 1843 she made a better fist of Abigaille at Parma, with Verdi spending much of the season in the town – at least partly on her account, though at this stage they appear to have been no more than friends; he was also busy arranging the dedication of *Lombardi* to the Duchess of Parma, his own sovereign. Strepponi managed only a few more appearances; she retired at thirty, and decided to make the best of a bad job by teaching in Paris, where rich pupils could be found. When she and Verdi met again she had been there for a year.

A chief cause of wear and tear on her voice was her readiness to sing five times a week or more – she once sang the heavy part of Norma six times in one week – and to fill every bit of the operatic calendar with engagements: feats most contemporary singers of her quality tried to avoid. Worse still, as she took on this schedule she went through a series of pregnancies – at least three, possibly four. Though a fair number of people around the theatre knew about the pregnancies, Strepponi and her friends and fellow-workers hushed them up; they honoured the first commandment of nineteenth-century morality, avoidance of public scandal.

While pregnant, Strepponi went on appearing till the last possible moment; unsurprisingly, she was often ill and exhausted, both before and after delivery. All this amounted to mismanagement of her career. True, for much of the time she was under contract to the impresario Lanari, who could engage her in this theatre and that; true too, she had to support a family from a young age. But her dealings with Lanari were spirited rather than canny; even as breadwinner she overdrew on her one asset, her voice. Altogether Strepponi, whose normal stance in later life was ironic poise, in this early phase showed a streak of recklessness.

Much has been written about Strepponi's personal life, her possible lovers before Verdi, and her children. What a short study can

9 Giuseppina Strepponi as Nina in Pietro Coppola's opera, which she sang in Venice in 1835–36 at the age of twenty. Contemporary engraving

attempt is to grasp her position within Italian society of the 1830s and 1840s, and what it meant for the man whose life she came to share.

As prima donna and head of household she was financially and legally independent – a state then open to very few women anywhere. Such a woman was not expected to behave just like a middle-class housewife, though up to a point she must heed middle-class convention. Women on the stage were part way through a long transition from the time (the seventeenth and early eighteenth centuries) when they were thought to be high-class prostitutes to that (the late nineteenth) when they could choose a middle-class standard of respectability and make it stick. In Strepponi's time some Italian women singers were described as 'of good conduct', but the need so to describe them shows that expectation still ran the other way. Those not 'of good conduct', all the same, by and large got away with it.

A touchstone is the career of Eugenia Tadolini, a prima donna six years older than Strepponi and just as famous. Daughter of a family 'better' than Strepponi's, she was – as everyone knew – separated from her husband, a minor composer twenty years older. Well after the separation she had two children by aristocratic Neapolitan lovers. A particularly mean-spirited impresario threatened to sue for damages because one of these 'husbandless' pregnancies had made her cancel a season, but for the rest she lived openly in Naples with her children and remained on good terms with her brother; whether she lived with her current lover is unclear, but the relationships were public knowledge. None of this seriously harmed a career of more than twenty years.

Could Strepponi have done the same? She lacked Tadolini's official married status, and only one of her lovers was a nobleman; how far these differences mattered is hard to gauge, because evidence of how other contemporary women artists managed their sexual lives is scant. The tone in which musicians and impresarios discussed these other women's love affairs – one of amused tolerance, only seldom tinged with contempt – suggests that with careful management Strepponi could have emulated Tadolini. As it was she ended virtually bereft of both children and career.

Her first child Camillino Strepponi, born in 1838, was the son of the theatrical agent and part-time impresario Camillo Cirelli. This man, at first Strepponi's common-law husband, went on acting as her professional adviser and friend through her later 'cheating, compromising affairs' as he called them; in 1843 he ruefully wished that she would leave them behind and think of her future. Cirelli did not legally acknowledge his son but helped to support him, certainly till he was eleven, perhaps later. When Strepponi in 1839 gave birth to a daughter, Sinforosa, Cirelli knew of her affair with a man he blamed as a 'vile seducer', probably a fellow-singer; he thought the 'good angel' Strepponi almost blameless, behaved like a forgiving husband, and accepted that he was the father on account of dates.[5] A possible stillbirth in 1840, and a further daughter, Adelina, born in 1841, are barely documented.

Who fathered these children matters less than what their mother did with them. She had Camillino brought up in Florence by her former maid; she herself visited seldom. When the boy was eleven she apprenticed him to a famous sculptor, who unhappily died soon afterwards; Camillino later studied medicine but died in 1863, aged twenty-five. Sinforosa and Adelina were immediately placed with working-class foster-families, the elder after a spell in an orphanage; they died, the one at eighty, the other at eleven months. Strepponi never saw the younger girl again; whether she saw the elder now and then we do not know. At all events she had no legal responsibility for either. The children's sex, we are almost bound to conclude, determined that one was looked after – in secret – and the other two discarded.

What did Verdi make of Strepponi's past? Perhaps not much. We know plenty about her attitude, almost nothing about his. Suggestions that *La traviata* alludes to Strepponi are wrongheaded: Verdi called Violetta a 'whore' (A, I, 503) – she was a kept woman – but Strepponi was an independent artist who supported a family. Her sexual life before the two of them came together was at once 'simple, natural' and, in the theatre, not uncommon – though probably worse managed than most.

At first he and Strepponi, with painful experiences behind them, may have been unsure of how long the relationship would last. In 1853, four and a half years after their Paris meeting, he allowed her for the first time to accompany him on business trips, something she had badly wanted to do, even if it meant, as she put it, seeing him no more than a quarter of an hour in every twenty-four. By the following year she was known in Paris, where they were again living, as Signora Verdi; Verdi turned back a letter addressed to her as Strepponi. By 1856, back in Italy, her handkerchiefs were embroidered 'GV', and by late 1857 Verdi wrote of her as 'my wife'.

Why then did they not marry until 29 August 1859? Tentative explanations have been put forward. Verdi may have wished not to be legally responsible for Camillino, who turned twenty-one in January 1859; or Strepponi may have contracted an earlier, secret, perhaps dubious marriage to a man who died about that time; or she may have felt unworthy. We do not know. The wedding, in a village church at Collonges in Savoy (then part of the new if still unofficial kingdom of Italy), was as secret as Verdi could make it: the only witnesses were the bellringer and the coachman.

Strepponi for many years felt overwhelming love and gratitude. By the time she and Verdi started living together she had become a fluent writer of letters and diaries in both Italian and French, with a little fractured English thrown in now and then; it is not always clear whether her intimate writings were meant for Verdi or only for herself. They tell us a great deal. Looking back, twenty years on, at their relationship – Verdi just then had shown himself irritable to excess – she recalled in her diary that on joining him she had 'wanted to become *a new woman*': she wished to respond worthily to the honour he had done her in making her his life's partner, and to the good 'this man' continually did her 'who, to be perfect, lacks only a little more gentleness and charm' (CV, 11, 37).

That, for a long time, was her only complaint about the man she called 'my Wizard'. When they were apart in the years up to 1853, she objected now and then if his letters were not warm enough: 'What the devil! Does one forget to love people at Busseto, and to write with a little bit of affection?' Still, everything at Busseto would suit her very well 'as long as you are there, you ugly, unworthy monster! [. . .] I detest and embrace you'. On a later occasion: 'Without you I am a body without a soul' (WalkerV, 195–6, 208).

Theirs was from the start a union of independent beings. She kept her own accounts and paid for her own clothes. One possible tie was ruled out. 'We shall' – she told Verdi in 1853 – 'have no children (since God, perhaps, wishes to punish me for my sins, in depriving me of any legitimate joy before I die).' The point of saying this was that Verdi should feel no need to overwork and make a lot of money, since there would be no one to hand it on to. Strepponi may have been aware that, to Verdi, handing on his name and fortune in fact meant a great deal, for she expressed the hope that he would not have children by another woman (WalkerV, 209). In 1868 the two of them were to adopt as their child and heir an eight-year-old Verdi girl cousin, Filomena Maria.[6]

Independent though each of them was, Strepponi for many years felt in Verdi's debt. In December 1860, when he was away and rain and solitude were getting her down, she wrote:

> the talisman that fascinates me and that I adore in you is your character, your heart, your indulgence for the mistakes of others while you are so severe with yourself, your charity, full of modesty and mystery, your proud independence and your boyish simplicity – qualities proper to that nature of yours, which has been able to keep a primal virginity of ideas and sentiments in the midst of the human cloaca! O my Verdi, I am not worthy of you, and the love that you bear me is charity, balsam, to a heart sometimes very sad, beneath the appearance of cheerfulness. Continue to love me; love me also after death, so that I may present myself to Divine Providence rich with your love and your prayers, O my Redeemer! (WalkerV, 226)

By the 1850s, as we can see, Strepponi was religious; she went to mass. That, in a Catholic country, did not necessarily make her unlike Verdi in her opinion of priests – who, if they followed the rules, must have withheld communion from her until the two of them were married.

Even with so many intimate papers to draw on, her personality eludes us. Frank Walker, who first published some of them, thought them 'witty', 'delightful', 'enchanting', 'beautiful'. There is another side. To her friend Caterina De Sanctis, whose newborn child had died, she wrote first with conventional solace (the child was better off in heaven) and then added: 'if you had no other children I should be a bit sorry for you, but as you already have a sufficient number of them and possess, too, a factory in full activity for the multiplication of the De Sanctis, I can't feel sorry for you at all' (27 March 1864, WalkerV, 248). Witty? Delightful? For her as for Verdi the parent–child relationship may have been fraught; unlike him, she lacked the means to vent her unconscious in parent–child duets.

Back in 1847–49, the tie between failed prima donna and rising composer benefited greatly from their living in Paris. He seems to have moved into a flat adjoining hers; not that it mattered, for when Verdi rejoiced in Paris as a city where no one bothered to point him out or gossip about him he meant, among other things, that he and Strepponi were left to get on with their lives. As a singer she was not quite finished: in 1847 she still gave occasional concerts, mainly in rich people's houses; she helped Verdi in private by singing and commenting on his melodies as he first sketched them. Her hand and his wrote out alternate lines in a duet for *Jérusalem*; as she was to do for the rest of her life, she drafted or helped to redraft some of his business letters, now and then smoothing out their asperities.

In Paris they were to live through revolution and the first stages of counter-revolution. By late 1847 much of Europe was in political ferment. In France the bourgeois monarchy of Louis-Philippe (who had just made Verdi a knight of the Legion of Honour) would be overthrown in February 1848. In Italy unrest had grown from 1843, when Vincenzo Gioberti's *Of the Civil and Moral Primacy of the Italians* first roused enthusiasm with its assurance that Italy could be great again and its proposal of an independent federation of the existing states under the Pope – enthusiasm perhaps all the greater because Gioberti's ideas were cloudy and his book unreadable. In July 1846 the election of the supposedly liberal Pope Pius IX led to bursts of public joy well beyond control; many assumed that the new reign would bring not just liberal reform in the Papal States and elsewhere but the fulfilment of Gioberti's vision.

Italy's was an extreme case of a general discontent with the authoritarian, unrepresentative state, characteristic of European middle-class and artisan groups and some aristocrats, all the sharper where, as in Italian towns, more and more young men could see little hope of jobs befitting their education and status; for the peasant mass, 1847 brought famine and slump. Among the educated the cry was for constitutional and representative government, seen as the key to a more modern society. Change of this kind must mean an end to the hegemony which, since 1815, Austria had exercised over the peninsula: though it upheld rational administration, the Habsburg empire had dug itself in as a conservative power opposed to any political reform. In Milan, Venice, and their territories Austria itself possessed an Italian state (called Lombardy-Venetia). Gioberti had skirted round this problem; in his independent federation, Lombardy-Venetia might perhaps have enjoyed autonomy under a Habsburg prince.

Verdi in his twenties, we have seen, gave signs of wanting a liberal republic, perhaps a democracy; he hated the authority that priests exerted over daily life. Such views easily went together with ideals of universal human brotherhood, of austere 'Roman' virtue, of an end to tyranny. We find them in Shelley's *Prometheus Unbound*, written in Italy in 1818–19; they have everything to do with liberation, not much with nationalism. But was not Verdi a nationalist longing for Italy to be united into a single state? Were his early operas not full of transparent appeals to fellow-nationalists? Until a short time ago everyone would have answered 'yes' to both questions. In fact the answers must be heavily qualified.

The Risorgimento – Italy's national 'resurgence' – was not a single-minded movement making steady progress towards unity. Conflicts abounded; moods, aspirations, and programmes changed; during the 1840s they changed almost from month to month – in 1847–48, from week to week. It is no use reading attitudes of 1844 or 1847 into an opera of 1842 like *Nabucco* or into what the audience made of it. Reading back, however, is just what goes on after a nationalist movement has triumphed. Though the movement has as a rule been the work of a minority, many people persuade themselves that they supported it all along. Rossini, after Italy had attained unity under King Victor Emmanuel II of Piedmont in 1859–61, wrote that he had always been 'warm for the fatherland' and for its freedom; he was probably sincere, yet, as his earlier letters show, the 1848 revolution in Bologna gave him such a fright that he moved away and, for years afterwards, abhorred popular movements and the modern world in general.

A prime example of reading back is the still common belief that the great choruses in Verdi's early operas, particularly 'Va, pensiero, sull'ali dorate' in *Nabucco* and its replication 'O signore, dal tetto natio' in *Lombardi*, gave voice to straightforward political nationalism; according to some late nineteenth-century writers, echoed by others ever since, they were wildly applauded by audiences otherwise barred from expressing their hope for a united Italian state. Roger Parker has now shown that in 1842–43 these choruses roused no special enthusiasm. This was still true even after revolution in 1848 had made nationalistic demonstrations welcome; some critics wrote off the choruses as not martial enough. Only after Italian unification did 'Va, pensiero' become an unofficial national anthem; reading back was so persuasive that Verdi himself came to believe the words of the chorus had led him to undertake *Nabucco* in the first place.[7]

Yet such choruses of yearning for a lost fatherland did express a cultural nationalism in which Verdi shared, as did many contemporary writers (though fewer musicians). Shame at Italians' fallen condition was bound up with hope that they might renew the past glories of their culture, and find within themselves a new energy and independence. Men and women who felt like this did not necessarily want a unitary Italian state, still less unity as it came about in 1859–61 – a takeover of the peninsula by the Piedmontese kingdom, the one Italian state with an independent army. Allegiance to one's own city or petty state was still strong; hence the welcome given to Gioberti's assurance that Italy could again become 'the leading nation' with no need for substantial change, let alone the total, self-sacrificing people's struggle for a unitary republic that the rival seer Giuseppe Mazzini had been preaching, as yet to a small minority. 'Va, pensiero' with its great swinging melody – most of it sung in unison – spoke for human brotherhood rather than for any nationalistic political design.

Almost down to the 1848 revolutions Verdi's operas enjoyed the patronage of the existing rulers; they could be given largely as Verdi and his librettists conceived them, because the censors appointed by the rulers saw little harm in them. Only in the last few months before the revolutions broke out did part of the audience adopt, for the first time, lines and scenes in the operas as triggers for demonstrations against the old governments; and only after the old governments had come back in 1849, far more reactionary for having been badly shaken, did Verdi have to cope with an obsessive political censorship.

In the years around 1840 Strepponi and Verdi did not behave like rock-hard nationalists. Strepponi in 1838 sang Norma in a gala performance at Cremona before the visiting Austrian emperor; no one applied the opera's theme of revolt to Italy's present situation, as some audiences were to do ten years later; the company lined up and sang a hymn in the emperor's praise, to loud cheers.[8] Verdi too celebrated the emperor's visit to his north Italian kingdom: he wrote a cantata to fulsome words by Piave, later a strong nationalist. In 1842–43 Verdi dedicated *Nabucco* to one Habsburg princess (later, such were the ambiguities of Italian politics, to marry the future Victor Emmanuel II) and took much trouble, spurred on by his late wife's anticlerical kinsman Demaldè, to dedicate *Lombardi* to another, his own sovereign Duchess Marie-Louise of Parma; he was moved when the duchess – an amiable and popular ruler – personally thanked him. Meanwhile Strepponi, singing *Nabucco* at Parma, was delighted with her honorary appointment as chamber singer to the duchess. Even in 1850, after the revolutions had failed, Demaldè lobbied Marie-Louise's successor to make Verdi a knight.

Censorship – carried out by Italian literary men in the employ of the various states – was political in that, as everyone knew, appeals to liberty and outcries against tyranny were unthinkable; certain words, for instance 'chains', acted as triggers. Librettists avoided them and before 1848 the issue was hardly a live one; revolts, as *Norma* showed, were acceptable if they happened in faraway times or places. What censors did mind was clergy or religious ritual on stage, behaviour opposed to Catholic morality, and personal allusions; their classical habit of mind made them dislike the serious treatment of 'low' or 'grotesque' subjects. The French Romantic plays and novels quarried by librettists abounded in most of these things.

Verdi none the less had little trouble. His librettists Solera and Piave censored their own work in advance; labelling Pope Leo the Great in *Attila* 'an ancient Roman' and omitting two of the three suicides at the end of *Ernani* was enough. The censor worried about possible liturgical gestures in *Nabucco*, but about nothing else in the work; the Archbishop of Milan had 'Ave Maria' cut out of *Lombardi* but in its place tolerated 'Salve Maria' (as well as the sacrament of baptism represented on stage); Piave lost some words about the Bruti and Gracchi – Roman republican leaders – from the conspirators' chorus in *Ernani*, 'Si ridesti il leone di Castiglia', but the chorus itself got through with its stirring call to renewed valour intact: as the courage and magnanimity of Charles V presently won over the conspirators the politics of the scene were impeccable.

Attila, the quintessential 'Risorgimento opera', passed the censor without remark and, it seems, without any demonstrations at the time (March 1846) of the first performance in Venice. The Roman general's line to Attila 'You shall have the whole world, leave Italy to me', later assumed to have been a nationalist rallying cry, puzzled some people; Verdi told Solera 'I understand what you mean' but asked for an explanation he could show (*C*, 440). When it came it – together with other details of the libretto – suggested that Solera shared Gioberti's vision. He had amended Werner's German tragedy to make the line more explicit; it now asked Attila as conqueror of the Roman empire to be in effect Italy's distant overlord (like the latter-day Austrian emperor?). From Verdi's words to Solera we might think that he too at that point shared the excitement over Gioberti's book. Other 'nationalist' passages in *Attila* were compliments to the old Venetian Republic, suppressed by Napoleon fifty years earlier; the Venetians still held to it so strongly that in 1848 they were to rise in its name.

Over all these works Verdi faced the censors of Lombardy-Venetia, the most reasonable in Italy. Those of Rome and Naples were far more obscurantist. There the heroine of *Giovanna d'Arco* – still accounted a heretic – turned into one Orietta, from Lesbos. Verdi was to face worse trouble of this kind later on. Local bigwigs and theatre owners could be fussier still: the mayor of Venice had a Christian hymn cut out of *Attila*; in the same city the noblemen on the executive committee of La Fenice would not give the first performance of *I due Foscari* – it showed two of their fifteenth-century predecessors in a bad light; their chairman demurred at having on stage in *Ernani* so unclassical an object as a horn – it had never been seen at La Fenice before; Verdi replied 'Well, this time it will be' (BM, 124).

Verdi's works of the 1840s were, all the same, 'Risorgimento operas'; the recent thesis that Verdi as Risorgimento bard is a myth (and so is the Risorgimento itself)[9] makes shrewd points but fails because it does not properly take in the music. Though the music has no specific political thrust, its energy and grandeur are the work of a man who needs in imagination to fling himself and his listeners into heroic action. Muddled, often contradictory as their behaviour was, enough Italians felt the same for us to talk of a Risorgimento, and of Verdi as its – not always conscious – prophet.

The best-known legend of Verdi as nationalist icon is the cry 'Viva VERDI' (with the composer's name an acrostic standing for 'Victor Emmanuel, king of Italy'). This was indeed heard – for a few weeks at La Scala from January to March 1859, the immediate run-up to the second, decisive war of independence. It was a wheeze limited in time and audience rather than the popular slogan read back into it after unification.

Verdi spent almost the whole of the 1848–49 revolutionary period in Paris: not at first glance a token of irresistible commitment to Italy.

He took a keen interest in early Parisian happenings – largely nonviolent – and witnessed them whenever he could. News of the revolutions all over Italy did fire him with enthusiasm, particularly news of the five days' rising in which the Milanese threw the Austrians out of the city. For a while he shared Mazzini's vision of a people's revolt that would bring about a united Italian republic. On 21 April 1848 he was back in Milan; to Piave (a volunteer soldier) he wrote:

> Honour to the whole of Italy, which at this moment is truly great!
> The hour of its liberation has struck, be sure of it. It's the people that want it; and when the people want something no absolute power can withstand them [...]
> Yes, yes, only a few years more, perhaps a few months, and Italy will be free, united, republican.

No point now, he wrote, in talking about music – the only apt music was that of the guns. In something of an anticlimax, the letter went on: 'I must go back to France to deal with commitments and with business' – that is, to write two operas and collect various sums due to him, too large to ignore (A, 1, 745).

The reason why the sums were too large to ignore was also the reason why Verdi was in Italy: it was to buy land around Sant'Agata, the place his ancestors had come from; he needed all the money he could lay hands on. A little earlier, still in Paris, he had expressed astonishment that some letters of his should have gone astray: 'I do realise that there's a revolution going on, but what have letters to do with it?' (C, 464). Verdi's enthusiasm was sincere; but neither revolution nor the ill-fated war of independence against the resurgent Austrian army took first place in his life. He spent the month of May buying his estate and at once went back to Paris.

There he was in time to witness the 'June days' – the bloody counter-revolution that crushed the rising of the Paris working class; the irremediable split among those who had acted together in February was to run, one way or another, through all the European movements that had likewise started in idealistic hope. By August the war in northern Italy was halted by defeat and armistice; with the rest of the peninsula in turmoil and constitutional government on the ebb Gioberti's illusory hopes had crashed. 'What a wretched pygmy epoch!' Verdi lamented to his nationalist friend Clarina Maffei, now in temporary exile from Milan, 'Nothing great: not even crimes!' (A, I, 757).

Venice still held out, and Rome, where, Pius IX having fled, Mazzini was to head a republic from February to July 1849. After meeting the venerated Mazzini in April 1848 Verdi had agreed to write a national anthem, a task of the sort he normally declined; it did not catch on then or later. He had a commitment to write an opera for Naples, and tried out several patriotic subjects, but Naples had again fallen to reaction; disturbances and economic crisis virtually paralysed theatres over most of the peninsula. In the end Verdi wrote La battaglia di Legnano for Rome and, just before the republic was proclaimed, went there to finish and rehearse it. A crowd broke into the dress rehearsal, a packed house acclaimed the first night, other patriotic demonstrators filled the streets outside. Once again Verdi spent just over a month in Italy, and then went straight back to Paris.

As the occasion demanded, Battaglia was Verdi's one openly nationalistic work. Its theme, the revolt of north Italian cities against the Emperor Frederick Barbarossa, could be applied to current events. Even then its tale of private emotion – a classic triangle – had originally fuelled a story with a French setting. When all the Italian constitutional governments fell (except Piedmont) Verdi agreed to recycle it in yet another version, bowdlerised and set in Holland during the revolt against Spanish rule; he did remark 'to keep [in the work] all the ardour for fatherland and liberty without ever mentioning fatherland or liberty is a mighty hard task', but added 'all the same, one can try' (A, II, 274). With a new harmonic refinement learnt in Paris, Battaglia lacks the thrust and unity of feeling of Ernani. It even-handedly distributes its grandiose choral finales between Barbarossa's side – a granitic Verdian bass, his army and supporters arrayed behind him – and the Italian threesome, reconciled as the tenor dies to a characteristic soaring melody on the words 'whoever dies for the fatherland cannot be evil-minded'.

Within less than six months of the first night, French troops overthrew the Roman Republic: the future Napoleon III, at that time president, had found this bait for the French Catholic vote. Venice too was starved out. Reaction had won everywhere. By November 1849 Verdi was disgusted. 'Italy', he wrote to his Paris publisher, 'is no longer anything but a vast and beautiful prison [. . .] to the eyes – a paradise: to the heart – an inferno!!' (WalkerV, 198).

He was once again back in Italy, this time for more than a fleeting visit. He and Strepponi at first moved separately, he to Busseto in early August 1849, she to Florence, where she dealt with Camillino's apprenticeship and with her investments. She then joined Verdi at Busseto in mid September.

There they settled into a town house Verdi had bought four years earlier. Of all places where they might have lived this one left Strepponi worst exposed to gossip and the cold shoulder. Paris had been ideal; if they had stayed Verdi could have gone on writing operas for Italy, as Donizetti had; he himself had just composed *Corsaro* and most of *Battaglia* there. Life in Milan or Florence, much smaller cities, would have been more exposed but – the example of Eugenia Tadolini suggests – almost certainly manageable. Busseto was a tiny place where Verdi's house, Antonio Barezzi's, the collegiate church, and the town hall were all within a couple of hundred yards of each other; everyone there knew Verdi and some resented him.

His father-in-law Barezzi had met Strepponi in Paris in the winter of 1847–48; they had liked each other, and on getting back to Italy the old man sent greetings through Verdi to 'Signora Peppina'. It was another matter to have her and Verdi sharing a house along the street. Barezzi himself was a lovable man, but his sons appeared to Strepponi – at times to Verdi as well – officious and unhelpful. Verdi's own father, a strict Catholic, seems to have disapproved. In the outcome Strepponi had to live from September 1849 to April 1851 virtually shut up in the Busseto house, an object of curiosity or scorn, most of the time with Verdi and the servants. While Verdi was away putting on a new opera in Naples or Trieste or Venice she may have gone off on a visit to her mother and sister, but at times she must have been on her own with the servants. When she went to church the congregation ignored her.

Why did Verdi do it? While Strepponi was still attending to business in Florence he wrote that if she disliked Busseto he would 'have her accompanied' to some other place. She chid him for the phrase; to be with him was enough for her. This proposal – as far as we can tell – showed not that their relationship was still doubtful but that Verdi understood the difficulties his companion would run into in Busseto. About his 'utterly charming home town' he had no illusions: 'How beautiful! How elegant!' he wrote ironically to one of his aristocratic women friends, 'What a place! What society!'[10] In leaving Paris Strepponi had burnt her boats; she was committed to Verdi; she was, we may guess, ready to take the consequences. Among these was to be her and Verdi's lasting estrangement from the town.

The broadside Verdi sent Antonio Barezzi is well known. In January 1852 he had just gone to Paris without entrusting his affairs to the Barezzis. His father-in-law, it seems, complained (in a letter now lost) that Verdi had cut himself off too drastically both from the town and from his own efforts to help. Verdi made his displeasure clear. He allowed for Barezzi's having been influenced by

> a town where people have the bad habit of prying into other people's affairs and of disapproving of everything that does not conform to their own ideas. It is my custom not to interfere, unless I am asked, in other people's business and I expect others not to interfere in mine [. . .] What harm is there if I live in isolation? If I choose not to pay calls on titled people? If I take no part in the festivities and rejoicings of others? If I administer my farmlands because I like to do so and because it amuses me? I ask again: what harm is there in this? In any case, no one is any the worse for it.

He then conceded that he would still rely on Barezzi for help with minor matters. Though Barezzi had clearly not dared mention his private life, Verdi went on ('since we are by way of making revelations'):

> I have nothing to hide. In my house there lives a lady, free, independent, a lover like myself of solitude, possessing a fortune that shelters her from all need. Neither I nor she owes anyone at all an account of our actions. On the other hand, who knows what relationship exists between us? What business connections? What ties? What claims I have on her, and she on me? Who knows whether she is or is not my wife? And if she is, who knows what the particular reasons are for not making the fact public? Who knows whether it is a good thing or a bad one? Why should it not be a good thing? And even if it is a bad thing, who has the right to ostracise us? I will say this, however: in my house she is entitled to as much respect as myself – more even; and no one is allowed to forget that on any account.

Verdi ended by threatening to leave a town which – the everlasting sore point – once 'did not consider me worthy to be its organist' and which now objected 'wrongly and perversely' to his conduct (WalkerV, 203–5). In this letter he 'revealed' nothing. On the contrary, its point was to assert the right to a wholly private life. There was, all the same, a price to pay; Strepponi paid most of it.

The answer to the question 'why did Verdi make her pay this price?' is clear. He was in Busseto because he wanted to settle down in his own landed estate – and that estate had to be not (as would have been perfectly possible) in some other part of Italy, it had to be where Verdi's ancestors had been tenants at least as far back as the seventeenth century. Such was his overmastering passion.

Verdi himself made it clear that he had not gone to Sant'Agata for the scenery. 'A horrible, isolated village', 'you couldn't find a place uglier than this', he told his friends from time to time (C, 498, 572). Like other irrigated plains – Holland, the East Anglian fens, the Bengal delta – the north Italian plain strikes many as ugly, but some as extraordinarily beautiful with its wide skies, vines (until recently) strung along rows of pollarded mulberries, horizons broken only by poplars or the odd spire, and, on a clear day, prospects of distant hills. True, the climate can be trying: cold, often foggy in winter, steaming hot in summer. From 1860 occasionally, from 1866 regularly, the Verdis would spend winters in Genoa – to begin with an unpolluted Riviera city – and part of the summer at an Italian watering-place.

Verdi bought land after one of his operas had scored an exceptional hit. When, much later, the Genoa errand-boy who delivered his breakfast buns asked which of his operas he liked best he replied in dialect '*Rigoletto* and *Aida*, because they're the ones that brought in the money'.[11] These helped to finance two of his biggest purchases, in 1854 and 1875. Verdi might have added *Ernani*: a few months after its runaway success in 1844 he bought his first parcel of land, a farm of about sixty acres known as the Fleapit. The negotiations in May 1848 that brought him to Italy ended with his exchanging the Fleapit against three other farms and throwing in some 166,000 francs (£6,640), about 95,000 francs of it in cash and the rest in mortgages. His new estate, of some 260 acres, was not much bigger than an English tenant farm, but it was land that, properly irrigated, would bear intensive cultivation.

Verdi's early operas had made nothing like the amount he paid out. He went deeply into debt to various people from the surrounding area, one of them his own father. What *Ernani* had done in 1844, and *Macbeth*, *Masnadieri*, and *Jérusalem* in 1847, was to inspire him with confidence that he could go on earning at a rate such as to pay off the loans and mortgages. Though there would be awkward moments his confidence was soundly based.

After buying the three farms Verdi went back to Paris. He therefore installed his father as caretaker. The estate included a five room house which he later described with some exaggeration as a 'hovel'; his parents went to live there. Such was the arrangement Verdi and Strepponi found when they moved to Busseto a little over a year later. It did not work. By the winter of 1850–51 Verdi wanted to move into Sant'Agata himself, with Strepponi, and he wanted his parents to move out; they were to live in a small rented house a mile or so away.

This separation is easily misunderstood. It had long been the custom for an Italian adult male who had done well in life to 'emancipate' himself at some point from his parents through a formal document agreed and signed before a notary; lacking such an 'emancipation', he might be held liable – to an indefinite amount – for his parents' support. Before Verdi and his father could agree several months went by. They were clearly annoyed with one another, Carlo Verdi, probably, from a general sense that his son and his son's mistress were belittling him, Verdi because he heard that his father expected to be made administrator or tenant of Sant'Agata, something he was determined not to allow: *in the eyes of the world, Carlo Verdi has to be one thing, and Giuseppe Verdi another* (A, 11, 93–6).

Verdi for a while communicated with his father through the notary; at one point he complained of the violent 'scenes' Carlo Verdi was making, and refused to let his mother go on looking after the Sant'Agata chickens: he wanted undivided control. But although he himself described the business as 'painful' and 'shameful' it was not so unlike the awkward build-up to a rite of passage often found in Italian rural life: the parties may quarrel and even stop speaking to one another for a while, but family ties remain basic to their lives; in the end they reach an accommodation. To call it a grave crisis marked by 'ruinous dissension' suggests an impact deeper and more lasting than the squabble between father and son appears to have had.[12] In April 1851 Carlo and Giuseppe Verdi at length signed notarised agreements. Verdi paid off his outstanding debt to his father, gave him a pension of 1,800 francs (£72) a year, and provided him with a horse. The parents moved out at the end of the month; at the beginning of May Verdi and Strepponi took possession of Sant'Agata.

For the first couple of years they kept the Busseto town house as their base and, when they stayed at Sant'Agata, camped out. There was everything to do – on the farms, in the house, in the immediate surroundings where they wished to make a garden. The resulting works would take many years. Strepponi, writing sixteen years later, recalled that at one time and another they had slept and eaten in every room but the kitchen, cellar, and stable; during the 1859 war of independence they had entertained important people in a covered yard where nesting swallows flew in and out. The making of Sant'Agata, house, garden, and estate, was to occupy most of the remaining half-century of Verdi's life; it was his private masterpiece, in which – within the confines of house and garden – Strepponi had a large share.

During the family quarrel over the 'emancipation' Verdi's mother had been seriously ill. She died at the end of June 1851. Verdi was deeply shocked; at first he wept uncontrollably. Within weeks he was deeply involved in writing music that would always be central to his fame. The first part of his life was over. The many remaining years would show his mastery.

4 The people's composer, 1849–1859: *Luisa Miller* to *Un ballo in maschera*

When Verdi took over Sant'Agata, unencumbered with any of his relatives, he was six weeks back from an event that signalled his mastery, literally to the world. On 11 March 1851 *Rigoletto* had its first performance at La Fenice, Venice. It was a hit on an international scale far beyond any of Verdi's earlier successes; judged by the money standard that he, like other theatre people, applied, the 28,150 francs (£1,126) he made just from further Italian and German productions in 1851–52 put it into a new class. This would be true of his next two operas, *Il trovatore* (Rome, 1853) and, from its 1854 revival rather than from its failed launch in Venice in 1853, *La traviata*. 'If you go to India and to the interior of Africa you will hear *Il trovatore*', Verdi told a friend in 1862 (VI, 17). It was true.[1]

The quality of these operas apart, a chief cause of their success was the steam engine. Railways and steamships were opening up vast parts of the globe to settlement, trade, or colonisation by Europeans and Americans; these men and women delighted in Verdi's three operas of 1851–53 and made them the most popular ever, at least until Puccini's *La bohème* came along in 1896. Touring companies now reached Kansas City, Sydney, Valparaiso, and Cape Town; opera houses went up in Constantinople and the Azores; mining villages in Colorado, upriver townships in Argentina, cantonments on India's north-west frontier heard Verdi's music performed in concert by travelling musicians or by wind bands, whose sheet music had come off steam-driven printing presses.

Humbler technology played its part. From about 1840 the barrel organ let Italian boys grind out 'La donna è mobile' to passers by in Manchester or Glasgow streets, many of whom never set foot in that ungodly, luxurious place the opera house. The accordion – known early in the century, with cheap versions available from about 1870 – took Verdi's melodies into the tavern, the cattle range, and the back porch. City populations that trebled or quadrupled through industrial growth brought hundreds together in choral societies, many of them – in Latin countries especially – devoted to 'Va, pensiero' and the Anvil Chorus. Where white men ruled, Verdi became the people's composer.

If he had earned a royalty each time a band or a barrel organ played a tune from the ever-popular three he would have become a millionaire. Thirty years on, in 1882, he protested against newspaper talk of his 'immense riches': '*Immense?!!* How could they be? [. . .] when I wrote a lot, operas were poorly paid; now that they are well paid, I scarcely write at all' (VR 82–85, 61). As so often, Verdi skated over crucial information but, in a rough and ready way, he spoke the truth. Though rich, he was never the Andrew Lloyd-Webber of his day.

What he failed to say was that his own shrewd grasp of changes in international law had seized an opportunity. He was the first Italian composer to understand that a treaty of 1840 between Austria and Piedmont, soon followed by others with the central Italian states, had at length brought about enforceable copyright: each of these states agreed to uphold on its own territory rights established in one of the others.

True, habits of piracy were ingrained: it took years, and iron vigilance by music publishers, to make copyright in a new opera stick. By the mid 1850s the battle was largely won in the heartlands of Italian opera: a successful work could now earn a hiring fee every time it was put on anywhere in north and central Italy, or in Vienna or Prague.

Southern Italy went on its old piratical way until Garibaldi conquered it in 1860. Piecemeal agreements among other west European states left some anomalies; in 1856–57 Verdi lost a suit in the Paris courts against the impresario of the Italian opera house, which was giving *Rigoletto* and *Traviata* from pirated material. Even the Bern Convention, which in 1887 finally harmonised the law over much of the world, still left out important operatic markets like Russia and Argentina – as Verdi was at once made aware by a pirate performance in Buenos Aires of his new work *Otello*, just ahead of that authorised by his publisher Ricordi.

Back in 1846, Verdi had resolved that – unlike earlier Italian composers – he would insist on having his operas performed as written. In spring 1847 he negotiated a contract with Ricordi that turned upside down what had until then been the normal terms for a new opera. Instead of receiving a large flat fee for the original production, and smaller fees from the outright sale of hiring and publishing rights, he would – for what became in 1849 *La battaglia di Legnano* – content himself with a flat fee of a mere 4,000 francs. He would, however, get 12,000 francs for the Italian publishing rights, and a smaller fee each time such rights were sold on to a foreign publisher. Most significant, he would get a fixed amount whenever the manuscript score and parts were hired out to a theatre. Verdi thus took advantage of the new copyright to make a successful Italian work do what successful French works did – pay year in year out.

Even then it took years to refine the terms of the agreement. Repertory opera – the habit of performing again and again a few successful works – was so novel in 1847 that Verdi agreed a limit on the hiring-out arrangements of ten years, no doubt thought to be their useful life; after 1865 this was extended to forty years, the copyright term set by a new Italian law. Ricordi persuaded him that a fixed hiring fee was too rigid; from 1850 Verdi therefore took a percentage, which over the years climbed from 30 per cent to 50 per cent of both hiring fees and sales of printed music and librettos. (An Italian composer generally bought the libretto of an opera outright at a low fee of 1,000 francs or so; to get round the French law that gave the librettist half the royalties Verdi eventually bought out the French librettos of *Trovatore* and *Aida* – a shrewd bargain.)

The first opera to which the new terms applied, *Battaglia*, fared poorly. They did not, alas, apply to Verdi's next opera. He had contracted as far back as 1846 to write an opera for Naples, on the old terms: he agreed to sell all the rights for a flat fee of 3,000 ducats (about 13,000 francs), far less than he would achieve a few months later with *Macbeth*. Largely because of the 1848 revolutions the opera was put off until autumn 1849. Verdi was understandably irked at having to write on terms he had left behind. He tried his best to get out of the contract or to alter it on the lines he had adopted in 1847, but the Naples management held him to it. Though he complied – as he asserted – only out of regard for the librettist, Cammarano, he gave full value: *Luisa Miller*, based on *Intrigue and Love*, Schiller's drama of a modest family crushed by absolute power, achieved a new intimacy and warmth of feeling. It would probably be heard more often today if it did not sound in retrospect like a partial sketch for *La traviata*.

Verdi was again understandably angry when the Naples impresario sold on all the rights to Ricordi, and when Ricordi in turn authorised a French version that would bypass both the composer (not a penny would come his way) and his usual, trusted Paris publisher Escudier. The fuss Verdi kicked up at length won him a quarter of the French rights as well as a percentage for Escudier. His arguments were dubious: he claimed to have sold the Naples impresario the rights in an Italian, not a French opera, and he accused Ricordi of having tried to bamboozle him by getting him to sign a document he had not properly read – a lapse hard to credit in this most businesslike of composers.

A further dispute blew up in 1855 over the rights in the French version of *Trovatore*, which would for many years earn royalties from the French provinces and Belgium. Verdi's contract, of the new, post-1847 type, gave Ricordi a share, but he insisted that as he had put in all the work on the new version he must enjoy all the rights.

To get his way he raked up other grievances, down to misprints in his published works. Ricordi might be within his legal rights – this was the nub of the matter – but he, Verdi, had 'done, over and over, far more than I had to: I who am very largely the source of your colossal fortune!' His complaint broadened out to include all his business dealings:

> Throughout my – by now lengthy – career I have always found impresarios, publishers &c &c harsh, inflexible, ever inexorable, if need be brandishing codes and law books. Always fair words and very bad deeds. Altogether I have never been looked upon as other than an object, a tool to be used as long as it produces something. Sad but true. (C, 168)

The world of Italian opera management and publishing was indeed harsh; but Verdi gave as good as he got. In this particular crisis he ended by buying out Ricordi's share; with a negotiator's virtuoso touch, he won a clause that reduced the publisher's 10,000-franc compensation by 2,000 francs if (as happened) the original-language production of *Trovatore* in Paris brought in less than expected. In all this Verdi's keenness to buy land at Sant'Agata and his anxiety over the debt incurred played a large part.

If mid nineteenth-century economic progress did a lot to spread the fame of Verdi's three most popular works, the mid nineteenth-century political reaction that swamped the continent of Europe gave him a lot of trouble in piloting his operas on to the stage – far more than he had had before 1848. Censorship was now fiercely political as well as moral and religious; nor had the censors given up their old classical prejudices.

Just as, in 1848, he had failed to understand why revolution might disrupt the post, so in 1850, after the revolution had collapsed, Verdi was slow to realise how tough the censorship had become. Nothing else can explain his choice of a libretto as provocative as *Stiffelio*: the French play it was based on showed a modern-day Protestant minister publicly forgiving his unfaithful wife by reading out at the climax of a church service Jesus's words to the woman taken in adultery – for Catholic Italy, a pile-up of taboos. Verdi rightly insisted that the hero must be a clergyman and his wife must challenge him to confess her, even after the censor had shorn the original production of all signs of the man's cloth: 'there is now', he complained, 'no character, no situation, no drama' (BM, 270–1; C, 108–9).

He may have been fooled by Ricordi's decision to give the first performance in Trieste: the city lay in the hereditary lands of Austria, where the Habsburgs had imposed tougher discipline on the Catholic Church than they ever ventured in their Italian possessions; when, three weeks after the first night, Verdi proposed *Stiffelio* to the owners of La Fenice, Venice, he suggested asking the imperial government in Vienna to licence the original text. He did not realise that 1848 had given that government a thorough fright: even within the Austrian lands it was moving towards a concordat with the Church, now seen as a breakwater against change, that would largely undo the old policy of state control.

Stiffelio was so hopeless in the conditions of the early 1850s that Verdi literally dismantled it: he cut up the autograph score and, in 1857, recycled it as *Aroldo*, with a crusader hero, the story removed to eleventh-century Kent and Loch Lomond, and some of the music changed. Lacking as it still did a Protestant minister, hence 'character, situation, and drama', it was no more successful. In recent years the original *Stiffelio* has found its way back to the opera house; with a robust tenor who can convey spiritual authority and complex feeling – a tall enough order – it impresses.

For Verdi the making of *Stiffelio*, his forgotten opera, was interwoven with that of *Rigoletto*, one of his most successful. In getting Piave to make a libretto out of Hugo's play *Le Roi s'amuse* he brought to a paradoxical climax his long sustained attempt to base an opera on *King Lear*. Where a *Lear* opera would have strained the resources of mid nineteenth-century Italian opera *Rigoletto* tested to the limit the tolerance of the censors.

Verdi's involvement with *Lear* did not begin or end here. He had brought it up in 1843 and again in 1848; in February 1850, just ahead of the contract for what would become *Rigoletto*, he looked to entice the tradition-bound Cammarano with a summary of a possible *Lear* opera, commenting that it must be handled 'in a wholly new manner, on a vast scale, without the slightest regard to convention' (C, 478–82). Between 1853 and 1857 he was to commission and then chew over with another writer, Antonio Somma, an actual libretto. Yet he never got round to composing the opera; when Somma produced a new draft Verdi countered 'something is lacking' – he could not say what; conditions for making a start were never right.[2]

Lear as an Italian opera did raise obvious difficulties: too many leading characters (the parallel story of Gloucester eventually had to go), the unlikelihood of finding at one go singers who could do justice to Lear, Cordelia, and the Fool, and – as Gabriele Baldini argued – the pointlessness of vying with Shakespeare's own music. Verdi's instinct perhaps told him to keep off. Yet he fastened on *Lear*-like moments in several of his operas – nowhere more than in *Rigoletto*: the intense relationship between a father humiliated and a daughter lost and found means that if Verdi had set *Lear* he would have had to repeat himself, something he always did his best to avoid.

In proposing *Le Roi s'amuse* Verdi knew that he might run into trouble: he asked the owners of La Fenice to clear the story with the authorities; he accepted Piave's assurance that it would get through and later complained of having been misled.

The French government had banned Hugo's play from the stage after the first night (it remained available in print). As an Italian libretto it raised many hazards. A plot to kill a king was specially unwelcome amid the reaction from the upheaval of 1848; so was a king who beds his subjects' wives and daughters and chooses to spend the night with a prostitute in a low dive. Even if a libretto cut the notorious business with the key, it could hardly leave out the climax of the work, when the courtiers hold the distraught father back from the door behind which his daughter is at that very moment being ravished. Nor could it leave out the solemn curse from one outraged father that comes to haunt another: mid nineteenth-century moral and religious propriety flouted as well as political. Aesthetic conservatives scouted a hero who was at once a malevolent buffoon and a loving, injured father, who was, besides, a hunchback, and who ended by lugging a corpse on stage in a sack: by classical standards, buffoon, hunchback, and sack were all intolerably 'low'.

Sure enough, the Venice chief of police (an Italian) came down with a total ban on a libretto of 'revolting immorality and obscene triviality' (C, 487). The owners of the theatre concurred. Their city, after the 1848–49 siege, was economically ruined; many of them were so straitened as to give up their boxes; they agreed to open La Fenice in 1850, and again in 1851, only because the imperial delegate (an Austrian noble) and the mayor (a Venetian noble) delivered an extra subsidy – paid for by the Venetian consumer. These authorities, however, were not quite as fierce as they made out. They wanted an opera season; they badly wanted a new Verdi opera. To begin with they tried to get most of their own way: at their suggestion Piave rewrote the libretto so as to cut out all the hazards just mentioned, down to the sack.

Verdi stood his ground. The ruler, he said, must be a libertine and act like one – else there would be no drama. As for the buffoon, the hunchback, and the sack,

> What does the sack matter to the police? Are they worried about the effect it will produce? Permit me to ask: why do they think they know better than I? [. . .] Finally, I see [the hero] has been made no longer ugly and hunchbacked!! Why? A singing hunchback, some may say! And why not? . . . Will it be effective? I don't know; but if I don't know, neither, I repeat, does whoever proposed this change. In fact I think it splendid to show this character as outwardly deformed and ridiculous, and inwardly passionate and full of love. I chose the subject for these very qualities and these original strokes; if they are removed I can no longer set it to music.

His notes, he added, 'good or bad as they may be', were not composed at random: he always set out to 'give them character', that is, to fit them to the dramatic situation. As things stood, however, 'an original, powerful drama has been turned into something commonplace and dead' (BM, 232–3). Verdi aligned himself wholly with the Romanticism that looked for truth in the collocation of 'high' and 'low', sublime and grotesque.

His protest was dated 14 December: with the season about to open in less than a fortnight, time pressed. The theatre owners and the authorities reached a compromise that gave Verdi most of what he wanted; he, Piave, and the owners' secretary, meeting at Busseto on 30 December, endorsed it. The king became a ruling duke (of Mantua, a state and dynasty helpfully extinct); the authorities in effect capitulated over the hunchback, the sack, and the original characteristics of Hugo's play; Verdi accepted some haziness about just what brought the ruler to the low dive. The Habsburg censorship, as usual, showed itself far more reasonable than those of Naples and Rome: in Naples till 1860, in Rome till 1870, *Rigoletto* had to masquerade under three other titles, with never a buffoon, a hunchback, or a sack.

The delay incurred in Venice none the less meant putting off the first night until 11 March. After having earlier gone through several changes of name and title the jester and the opera both settled down to that now familiar; as Rigoletto, Felice Varesi – the original Macbeth – was still (just) able to give the part the Shakespearean resonance Verdi found in it.

On first hearing that the subject might be turned down Verdi had protested that, trusting in Piave's word, he had 'got down to studying it and thinking about it deeply, and in my mind I had arrived at the idea, the musical colour [tinta]'; if he now had to turn to another story he would not have time for such essential preparatory work, the most exacting part of his task (BM, 209). This meant that – as he usually did – he had started sketching musical themes, some perhaps attached to a few words, and working out the overall movement of a scene. More fundamentally, by 'idea', *tinta*, and – yet another term he applied to his work on *Rigoletto* – 'intentions', Verdi meant that he sought to give each opera its own individual, unmistakable character and unity.[3] Just how he did this exercises modern scholars perhaps more than any other aspect of his art.

Verdi was conscious almost from the start of wanting a unity his predecessors had not looked for: though they might now and then achieve it unawares, to Rossini, Bellini, and Donizetti an opera was a string of numbers, each with its own character and appeal. As early as 1843 Verdi urged on his librettist (over *Ernani*) by writing 'when I have a general idea of the libretto as a whole I can always find the notes'; as it turned out he need not wait until he had got Piave's full text, for the 'idea' of Hugo's play so fired him that he was able to start sketching (BM, 70, 93–4). Much later, reacting in 1868 to a foolish statement in which the Minister of Education of united Italy held up Rossini as the country's one musical glory, Verdi observed that Rossini and his followers lacked 'that golden thread that binds all the parts together and, rather than a set of numbers without coherence, makes an opera' (CV, II, 28).

Already in 1851 he wished that an opera could be 'a single number', without arias, duets, choruses, and so on. This should not be taken literally. It meant not that he hankered after 'unending melody' as in late Wagner; nor did he always want to get away from 'a set of numbers' – when his librettists offered him unorthodox layouts (for *Trovatore* and *Un ballo in maschera*) he himself put 'numbers' back in. Rather it meant that he sought a text at once original and – somehow – unified. *Trovatore* should be 'novel' and 'bizarre', the more novel and bizarre the better, but the 'golden thread' should run through it from beginning to end (A, II, 122–3).

How Verdi found the *tinta* or 'golden thread' is, on one level, a technical question a short book cannot go into. What creates it may be metre, tempo, the use of certain keys or modes (no Verdi opera, though, follows a systematic key plan), of certain pitches or rhythmic figures or instrumental timbres, of reminiscence themes, of melodies in arc-like or other characteristic form, all painstakingly devised in sketches as musical 'cells', modified, and then cunningly worked into the musical structure at crucial points in the drama. Those who wish to pursue the matter cannot do better than read Pierluigi Petrobelli's *Music and the Theater*. He sees *Macbeth* as the opera in which Verdi first achieved inner coherence – 'a complex, articulated system of "signs"

10 Two views of *Rigoletto*, Act 3.
(a) In the imaginary setting used as frontispiece of the original vocal score, Sparafucile's tavern is a modest building;

10 (b) Giuseppe Bertoja's original stage design: the prestige of the Teatro La Fenice demanded that the tavern should look implausibly grand

valid through the unfolding of the entire dramatic action': unobvious musical correspondences between the key murder and sleepwalking scenes mark 'the profound logic that determines the organisation' of this as of later scores and ensures their continuing impact on audiences today.

Rigoletto achieves inner unity even though Verdi felt able to use, for Gilda's innocent musing on her lover's name ('Caro nome'), a melody he had sketched for Stiffelio's wife – a conscience-stricken plea to her lover to end their adulterous affair. He left it out of *Stiffelio*; this (Philip Gossett has inferred) shows that his mind was already moving half-aware towards his next work: Gilda had intruded on Lina.[4]

Rigoletto's unity comes of a structure bold for its day, fraught with the passions of a singular, towering human being. Verdi himself wrote that he had conceived the opera 'without arias, without finales, with an interminable string of duets' (C, 497) – a near-accurate description. No one has a full double aria except the tenor (and we generally hear only the first part, 'Parmi veder le lagrime'; modern performances as a rule leave out the ensuing fustian cabaletta, though it is needed both on musical grounds and to show the duke moving from the sentimental to the cocksure). None of the three acts ends with an orthodox ensemble. As for the 'string of duets', they encompass a formidable range of emotion, shifting from moment to moment and unerringly true to character.

Verdi fines down still more the technique already at work in the *Macbeth* duet. He dovetails melodic sections, each at once conveying a change of mood; often he sets the two vocal lines against each other in contrast or comment. By such means either of the two Rigoletto–Gilda duets reaches a still centre of feeling, a moment of expansion such as Rossini had taught Italian composers to strive for; but where the middle sections of Rossini's duets (exemplified in *Semiramide*) keep the two voices meltingly together, Rigoletto's 'Veglia, o donna' and 'Piangi, piangi fanciulla' launch stepped melodies of a tenderness that offers hope or, in the midst of grief, solace; upon them Gilda enters – in the first duet with a bright key change, in the second with plangent interjections, in both with different short necklaces of semi-staccato notes that wonderfully convey her innocence; as in 'Caro nome' her coloratura, never showy, is an exhalation of youth. Both duets then discharge piled-up feeling in irresistible quick sections, father and daughter still differentiated until, in the second, 'revenge' conclusion, Rigoletto's vehemence carries all before it.

The climax of this musical-dramatic writing comes in the celebrated last-act quartet ('Bella figlia dell'amore'). Like Mozart's quartets in *Idomeneo* and *Don Giovanni*, it is a supreme, because lucid and economical, instance of opera's power to voice different emotions at once. We are accustomed to this unique power, but we are accustomed to it largely thanks to Mozart and Verdi.

'A string of duets' inadequately describes what happens, on the one hand in Rigoletto's great scene with the courtiers, on the other hand in the first and last scenes of the work.

By the scene outside the bedroom door the courtiers' music has already characterised them: the bouncy choruses so open to parody achieve a tone at once ironic and flash. Rigoletto's anxious search, his onslaught as he realises what is going on ('Cortigiani, vil razza dannata'), his plea to the one man he thinks open to compassion, his final grovelling to the whole body of courtiers transcend the routine aria structure; they do it by musical means. At the discovery 'the ascending gradient of the drama is exactly reflected in the music by changes of rhythmic texture, movement, and tonality', while in the main movement 'each stage in Rigoletto's abjection is marked by a further move to the flat side of the key'.[5] The accompaniments to begin with recall the busy, at times arbitrary patterns of the early operas, yet – uncannily apt – they shoulder the drama, in particular the 'weeping' figure that underlies the plea to Marullo; in the last section ('Miei signori, perdono, pietate') the cello solo guides the voice towards nobility in desolation. The scene as a whole shows Rigoletto as a tragic figure: 'Lear-like' is not far-fetched.

Verdi has prepared for it by giving his hero in Act I a soliloquy ('Pari siamo!') that reveals all at once the height and breadth of the jester's soul; it too voices Rigoletto's abrupt changes of mood by dovetailing short sections, punctuated with his haunted, monotone recall of the curse laid upon him. Just ahead of this formidable utterance, another cello, this time with double bass joined in eerie oscillation and soft woodwind-cum-pizzicato underlay, cradles Sparafucile's offer of a contract killing; though the layout comes from a Paris *mélodrame*, Verdi transmutes it into something at once night-shrouded and bizarre.

'Pari siamo!' had a precedent, Norma's tragic soliloquy in Bellini's opera. *Rigoletto*'s opening scene is something new in Italian Romantic opera, though it too goes back – to the ballroom scene in *Don Giovanni*. A rapidly shifting dance sequence bears forward conversational exchanges, with the duke's 'Questa o quella' a mere strophic flourish repeated; the brief concertato, Rigoletto's sneers, Monterone's denunciation and curse, are all vivid fragments of what in a conventional opera would have been fully developed numbers; the quarter-hour scene unfolds as continuous music drama.

The storm scene in Act 3 is more radical still. After the quartet Verdi throws away the Italian operatic book of rules. The storm breaks out from time to time in lone musical figures, interspersed with reminiscences of the quartet and of the duke's song: low, hollow chords, bafflingly drone-like, flecks of lightning (a skittering piccolo), humming wind sound (a wordless offstage chorus); at the height of the storm a formal, relentless short trio pits Sparafucile against his sister while Gilda overhears and, in a soaring phrase, makes up her mind to offer herself to the murderer's knife. Though Verdi here works in the required symmetry the effect is again of continuous music drama; it so grips the listener that he hardly notices the surviving armature of regular forms. In Gilda's dying assurance to her father those forms come back more obviously – in the delicate violin and flute accompaniment, beautifully.

Rigoletto shows Italian opera, 'that ultra-classical product of Romanticism', at high noon; the tension between freedom for drama's sake and regularity for form's sake propels it with inevitable-seeming shapeliness and force conjoined. One may easily share Vaughan Williams's regard for it as Verdi's greatest opera.

And 'La donna è mobile'? The barrel organ made it for years the one piece everyone knew and some despised. It is in fact a popular song, deliberately written to sound like one; thanks to Hugo as much as Verdi it works to powerful dramatic effect when Rigoletto hears in the distance the voice of the man whose corpse supposedly lies at his feet. Sung rather than bellowed, it confirms the duke's light-minded swagger, and falls into place.

The success of *Rigoletto*, a unique event in a time of reaction and economic crisis, fired Verdi to his most intense creative period. Between the spring of 1851 and the winter of 1852–53 he conceived, wrote, negotiated, and saw performed his other two most popular works; they had their first nights within less than seven weeks, *Trovatore* in Rome on 19 January and *Traviata* in Venice on 6 March 1853. Verdi did this at a time when he was anxious over Sant'Agata, the debts he had incurred to buy it, the quarrel with his father, his mother's death, his father's serious illness, and the gossip in Busseto over Strepponi. He was quarrelling with Ricordi over *Luisa Miller*; from January to March 1852 he negotiated in Paris a contract for a five-act grand opera; in the autumn and winter of 1852–53 he suffered from rheumatic pains. Nothing held him back.

The two operas look as though Verdi set out to write contrasting works – *Trovatore* conservative in its musical structure, its drama the quintessence of Romantic chivalric fable (though a current of formidable energy runs through both); *Traviata* on a contemporary, risqué subject, its music tinged with delicacy and intimate feeling and bringing back here and there the innovative 'string of duets' method. In fact the contrast seems to have been, at conscious level, unplanned: much of it came, first of Verdi's struggle with his librettist Cammarano over *Trovatore*, and then of his sudden choice of the *Traviata* story – to begin with hard for the Venice management and audience to accept.

Neither work gave Verdi trouble from the official censors, in part because he and his librettists as usual censored themselves. Everyone in the Italian opera business knew that you could not have, as in the wild Spanish drama from which Trovatore was hewn, a novice who ran away from her convent to join her lover, and that there would be difficulties about her later suicide; everyone was schooled in a convenient vagueness on such points – a vagueness kept strictly to word and gesture, while the characters' unbridled passions found full voice in the music. The source of Traviata, Alexandre Dumas fils's then brand-new play La Dame aux camélias, had already censored out the fairly realistic account of a courtesan's life given in his earlier novel; it had launched the consumptive, self-sacrificing heroine on the mythical path that would transform Marguerite into Violetta and then Camille, with many by-blows along the way. Yet in the few years running up to unification central and southern Italian states bowdlerised the opera still further; in Britain and America it met some resistance, particularly if it was to be given in English.

Verdi's main difficulties came from fellow-professionals and from opera management. He wanted novelty – something '*new, great, beautiful, varied* [. . .] as bold as possible, with *new forms*' (C, 531); they liked the familiar and safe – none more than Cammarano. His and Verdi's discussion (by post) of the Trovatore libretto shows a 'clash of two fundamentally different dramaturgical conceptions'.[6] Faced with García Gutiérrez's manic tale of witch-burning, revenge, and civil war, Cammarano sought to tidy it up into a good old love triangle, with no politics, clear motivation, the lovers respectably betrothed, a final mad scene with aria, and plenty of well-defined numbers along the way. The two men nearly quarrelled; Verdi's respect for Cammarano, however – confirmed when the poet died just after finishing the libretto – left most of this conventional structure unchanged.

One thing Cammarano had persuaded him to add was an introductory scene expounding the events of twenty years before – Azucena's notorious mistake when, to avenge the burning of her mother at the stake, she threw the wrong baby on the fire. Have audiences ever got this piece of news from listening to Ferrando's narration alone? It seems doubtful. Verdi, however, in the whiplash rhythm and 'primitive' notation of 'Abbietta zingara' gave them something better: he plunged them at once into Azucena's musical personality and into the whirl of extreme passions that is *Trovatore*.

Parodied, guyed, critically execrated, often thrown on to the stage with cardboard sets and no rehearsal, *Trovatore* was for the rest of the nineteenth century Verdi's most popular opera. It became the opera nearly everyone could recognise, the one the Marx Brothers disrupted and Danny Kaye blundered into, the quintessence of an extravagant genre. For some time past it has lost ground: troubadour knights and damsels in distress no longer mean much, nor do they bear updating as in the famous 'mafia' *Rigoletto* of Jonathan Miller's production; four star singers, besides, come dear. The best approach today is probably that of Gabriele Baldini, a scholar of Jacobean literature: he saw *Trovatore* as akin to Webster's tragedies, its four chief characters irrational and fleeting in their encounters, self-contradictory in their love and hate, pursuing their destinies to the death as though into the fire whose image runs through the work.

Verdi, without knowing Webster, seems to have thought of it like that. He chose the story for its wildness; he would have lost patience with modern conductors who try to make it 'reasonable'. When, after Cammarano's death, a young Neapolitan writer tidied up the libretto for him, Verdi was quick to lay down what he wanted. He demanded a new, leisurely aria ('D'amor sull'ali rosee'), but at the denouement he imposed speed. He himself slashed away at Cammarano's ending; only the barest exchanges survive as Di Luna has Manrico rushed off to execution and Azucena cries 'He was your brother!' A friend objected that Cammarano's words for Azucena were 'consequential' on her earlier behaviour. Verdi replied that he knew all about 'consequentiality', 'but the greater part of the drama [...] is summed up not in those words but in one word ... "Revenge!"' (CV, I, 10–11). No time for Manrico to have been beheaded? In the theatre it matters not at all. What counts is dramatic time; after the heights and depths of the work Verdi's whirlwind finish is right.

11 Giuseppe Bertoja's design for Act 1, scene 2 of *Il trovatore* at La Fenice, Venice

Trovatore's lasting fame was no accident. It is – Baldini and Petrobelli have shown – tightly organised both dramatically and musically. This organisation lies buried deep in the work; we are hardly aware of it as the total gesture sways us. What is plain is the relentlessness of the fast music, a match for the characters' anguish and defiance. Verdi's Italian contemporaries called him 'the maestro of fast tempi' (VI, 116); the trio confrontation at the end of Act 1 brings back the headlong élan of *Ernani*, more finely scored. Yet what makes this music often irresistible is not speed so much as rhythmic variety and surprise: Verdi was, in Carl Dahlhaus's words, 'before all else a genius of musical rhythm'.[7] The cabaletta sections of arias and duets spring at us, takingly fresh; if some of those involving Count Di Luna seem brazen in their accompaniments that may put the noble villain's pride in an ironic light.

Irresistible too are the famous popular numbers. The Anvil Chorus with its offbeat accents and ting-a-ling scoring is just what an exotic theatre tableau should sound like, the chorus 'Squilli, echeggi' just the bouncy tune an infantryman should march to and never forget. The Miserere, technically an extended middle section between the two parts of Leonora's Act 4 aria, brings off the theatrical coup in all opera – what this genre alone can do: no wonder it features in both the Marx Brothers and Danny Kaye films already mentioned. Verdi works together a hushed offstage chorus presaging death, in the orchestra a rhythmic figure embodying it, onstage the voice of a lone, desperate woman, then a man's voice, hidden, in lambent reassurance. The combination of a looming stage picture, of voices distanced in space, and of dramatic surprise comes from Parisian grand opera; Verdi here trumps it in spades.

Trovatore's highest distinction lives in the soloists' vocal line. It gives each of them immediate, unmistakable life. Leonora – an emblem of loving womanhood rather than a character – has again and again an arching line, each time different yet always an index of sacrificial nobility. It soars above the Act 2 finale, redeeming it from the need for a conventional slow–fast pattern; in the first section of both her arias ('Tacea la notte' and 'D'amor sull'ali rosee') the last lines of the stanza, as often in Verdi, heighten the feeling, but here voice and orchestra soar in glorious expansion, in the earlier, confident aria a seemingly endless fountain, in the later one more delicate, veiled in string and woodwind tone and haloed by a trill; in the final trio the voice discourses yet one more great arch before Leonora's death brings a magical harmonic twinge at the close. Coloratura always serves a dramatic purpose, melancholy in 'D'amor', passionate in its cabaletta 'Tu vedrai che amore in terra', hectic as Leonora strikes her bargain with the count.

Azucena's musical life has its soaring moments too, particularly when she utters her love for the man she calls her son, but her line more often turns obsessively round and round on itself; it does so almost throughout the scene with Manrico in which she lets slip the tale of her mother's burning and her own horribly botched revenge – not just in the formal parts (the song 'Stride la vampa', the narrative aria 'Condotta ell'era in ceppi', her share in all but the last part of the ensuing duet) but in her recitative descents into her low notes as she broods over remembered horror. She too, rather than a character, is a wandering emblem of obsession – with hallucinatory images of her mother's death and of what may await her alleged son, with the horror behind the visible world: she is perhaps another fragment of Lear on the heath. Only at the end, in prison under sentence of death, does obsession give way to something like Lear's awakening to Cordelia – the vision of peace in the hills with her son ('Ai nostri monti'), a glimpse of needed benediction before the end.

The men's vocal line is not quite so individual, but Manrico and Di Luna have the 'superb distinction' Shaw wrote of; the former shares much of Leonora's aspiring nobility and both share her elegance in arias that demand unremitting legato control ('Ah sì ben mio' and 'Il balen del suo sorriso'). To Manrico, the Verdian robust tenor in meridian splendour, is entrusted the cabaletta 'Di quella pira', the vocal equivalent of a stone shot from a sling – Verdi probably countenanced the unwritten high Cs; when performed as it should be it allows no one to ask 'Why not rush off and rescue your mother from the stake instead of singing about it?'

Trovatore summed up Italy's experience of high Romantic ardour. As in other parts of Europe, the failure of the 1848 revolutions brought a mood of conscious realism. It shattered the high hopes people like Verdi had entertained; at the same time it discredited the old order. Some, Verdi probably among them, began to hope for what seemed the only practical answer – the conquest of northern Italy by Piedmont, the one state left with a liberal constitution as well as an army.

A kindred interest in the artistic realism then making its way in France led him to choose *La Dame aux camélias* as the basis for his next opera. This time he would deal with a well-known contemporary figure, the Paris courtesan; the illness that killed her would be one – tuberculosis – specially virulent in the last few decades; her reason for making a heroic sacrifice of her one true love would be to save a bourgeois marriage in her lover's family; the money she ran through and her friends gambled with would be real 1853 money; as she lay dying a real 1853 doctor would feel her pulse.

All this was exactly what disconcerted the management and, later, the audience of La Fenice. Verdi had foreseen their objections: everyone, he recalled on 1 January 1853 while he was working on the score, had cried out at his proposing to show a hunchback on the opera stage; he implied that he would again brush aside 'ridiculous scruples' (BM, 306). In fact he had to give way.

We do not know what arguments the theatre owners used to overcome his insistence on a contemporary setting. The chorus, they alleged in an official statement – part-timers recruited, as was then usual in Italy, from among market women and artisans – would not have carried conviction as ladies and gentlemen of 1853, but could pass muster in the costumes of the period chosen, 'about 1700'. There may have been some truth in this; more likely, an opera showing courtesans, gamblers, and a respectable middle-class father, all in everyday crinolines and top hats amid 1853 furniture and medicine bottles, seemed too near the bone. Verdi may have felt in a weak position because rehearsing and launching Trovatore had made him late with Traviata and he was going to be late in reaching Venice. By 5 February he had agreed 'with great reluctance' – his librettist Piave reported after negotiating with him at Busseto – to a period setting. He still outlawed wigs; he no doubt wanted 1650 'cavalier' costumes rather than 1700 'Louis XIV' (BM, 316–17). In the event the singers appear to have worn wigs.

Piave had been sent post-haste to Busseto because on 30 January Verdi had threatened not to deliver Traviata at all; his reason was in part that he was suffering from his rheumatic complaint, but mostly that he had heard bad reports of all the La Fenice singers; he wanted the prima donna, Fanny Salvini-Donatelli, replaced by someone younger and more elegant. Piave found him in an 'infernal temper'; in the end he agreed to complete the opera and accept the singers as well as the period costumes, though he prophesied a 'total flop' (BM, 312–17). When Traviata opened, a mere eight days late, Salvini-Donatelli was the only principal to win applause and good notices, mainly for her coloratura in Act I; in the remaining two acts the baritone (Varesi, now in serious decline) and the tenor were in poor voice; the audience laughed.

Verdi, as was his way, registered the flop: 'Is the fault mine or the singers'? Time will tell' (BM, 326). It did. A little over a year later at the other, less prestigious Venice opera house, the San Benedetto, Traviata scored a resounding hit. Verdi had made some helpful changes – significant rather than extensive – but the chief cause was the new prima donna, Maria Spezia, young, frail, and convincing. The opera went all over the world; from then on Verdi remained convinced that it needed a singing actress, even one with a small voice, rather than a star vocalist.

Traviata is indeed, more than Rigoletto and Trovatore, essentially a theatre piece – its structure still classical, with the outline of a realistic prose drama showing and, here and there, bleeding through. Mixed in among wonderfully apt musical settings are passages that work above all as stage effects: the gipsies and toreadors at Flora's party, needed to afford a rest between two confrontation scenes; the tripping dance music that shows Violetta's friends to be at once manic and commonplace; the braying of carnival revellers outside her window as she lies dying. If the performance works these throw into relief the scenes that matter. At two crucial points in the last act Verdi stops the singing and takes to *mélodrame*: Violetta reads out the letter that announces (too late) Alfredo's return; then, on the point of death, she feels she is miraculously regaining strength. Spoken words accompanied by music (a reminiscence of Alfredo's Act 1 love song, present at other turning-points in the drama) make a powerful theatrical effect – undimmed by our knowing the device from countless films; but they make it by breaching the normal structures of Italian Romantic opera.

Obedience to those structures can throw up weak patches – the cabalettas for Alfredo and his father in Act 2, the former conventional, the latter hollow, both usually cut in performance; when they are left in for the sake of 'authenticity', the opera sags. Cabalettas sat ill to the demands of realism: that may explain Verdi's twice failing at the kind of dynamic movement he was expert in. Or he may just have composed too fast to get everything right.

Resort to *mélodrame* perhaps flowed from the demands of realism; it was not, however, what Shaw had in mind when in 1891 he called *Traviata* 'a much more real and powerful work than *Carmen*' – at that time the model of realistic opera.[8] What is real and powerful about it is emotion whose immediacy works through musical structure so fined down as to seem now and then epigrammatic. The libretto of *Traviata* is sentimental because it glosses over the truth about the courtesan's relationships, and colludes with social convention while weeping over her as victim; Verdi was perhaps reacting against this sentimentality as well as against the yet more edulcorated version put on in Rome when he wrote bluffly to a friend there 'a whore must always be a whore' (A, 1, 503). In fact his music communicates Violetta's inner life as genuine, delicate, and selfless, a feat Greta Garbo was later to bring off by other means in the film *Camille*.

The fining down comes in part of limpid instrumentation – just sixteen violins, divided, at the start of the two preludes, other delicate orchestral writing at crucial points elsewhere – in part of melodies that range within a small compass yet keep up great variety and character. This gives extra force to the music of passion when it breaks out in wider-ranging forms – overwhelmingly in Violetta's farewell appeal 'Amami, Alfredo', already heard in the Act I prelude, but also in her arc-like cry of distress, thrice repeated, during the scene at Flora's and her melting phrase over the great swinging ensemble at the end of it. Such expansive moments are short; their brevity helps to explain how *Traviata*, an opera about a woman who sacrifices everything for love, shuns all insistent eroticism. As an Italian critic has well put it,

> love, for Verdi, is always an active force, an emotion working itself out amid the other feelings that make up the complexity of the character; in fact it sharpens those feelings by entwining itself with them and spurring the character to action, yet it never takes over as the only motive, it never overwhelms that thematic complexity.[9]

By the time Violetta sings 'Amami, Alfredo' it comes as the passionate commitment to love of a whole person, rather than – as at climactic moments in Puccini – a vibrant cry from characters whose erotic life is their whole being.

Departures in Act 1 from the prevailing *tinta* of narrow-stepping melody serve to bring out Violetta's personality as it lives before she commits herself. They are also what makes the part fearsome: Verdi in this act imposes coloratura, now and then hazardous – the last time he does so – and then wants other demanding accomplishments in the two later acts. The prelude has already touched in her gentleness and the melancholy of her doomed existence. The toast in swinging triple time is as characteristic in its way as Lady Macbeth's: Violetta can still put a graceful sheen on the trivial world she dwells in; at the end of the second stanza her voice, dominating Alfredo's, shows her in control.

Not for long. After he opens the duet ('Un dì, felice') – the rests in the opening line mark the catch in his throat – he takes off into a declaration of all-encompassing love ('Ah, quell'amor'); this, the opera's recurrent theme, does not soar heavenward as Elvira's and Leonora's line did; it is intense, straightforward young love made emblematic. Violetta counters with teasing, leaping coloratura; the two sing for a while against each other, but as the short duet draws to its end her line first moves in counterpoint to his, then in descending melisma over his repetition of 'croce e delizia', until at length the two sing together, still melismatically: proof, by means only opera commands, that her heart has surrendered though she does not yet admit it; the Rossinian duet made into an epigram.

A yet more famous operatic coup ends the act. Left alone, Violetta muses: can this be the love she has always longed for? The simple, inevitable-seeming minor melody ('Ah fors'è lui') – another 'catch in the throat' in the opening bar – eases from minor to major, and the major is Alfredo's emblematic song. She then rejects the whole idea as impossible: forget love, back to the demi-monde and its febrile waltz, cue for cabaletta, fire off the coloratura in glinting streamers and spikes! Into 'Sempre libera', though, breaks Alfredo's song, this time in his own offstage voice (from the street? From Violetta's heart?); the two melodies contend with each other right to the fall of the curtain, yet there is no doubt of which has won.

The high point of Traviata is the long Act 2 duet in which Alfredo's father persuades Violetta to give him up. Verdi drives further the method used in Rigoletto to carry the two voices through a run of dove-tailed short movements. Each movement ferries their changing emotional responses; each speaks with extraordinary psychological truth – Germont's rhythmically insistent 'Un dì, quando le veneri', Violetta's breathless, desperate 'Non sapete', the purged, inward simplicity of her resolution and grief ('Dite alla giovine'). Nothing is forced; the voices stay for the most part within a short compass, that of civilised nineteenth-century people, yet their feelings are genuine and intense. The ghost of the triple time that pervades Violetta's world shows, transmuted, in her crucial movements, while – Carl Dahlhaus has written – the ghost of the Italian Romantic double-aria structure shapes the whole scene: 'the impression never arises of a mere string of emotions, paraded one after the other [...] the contrasting periods always relate to each other like dialectical, mutually complementary antitheses [...]'. Verdi here solved the problem of how to set dialogue in cogent form without resorting to 'musical prose'.[10]

Deep pathos veiled with discretion marks the last act – in the prelude with its sense of tears held back, in Violetta's aria after the reading of the letter ('Addio, del passato') – its last high note a stabbing sigh – in many of the recitative exchanges; as the heroine wastes away, her vocal resources allow her only the simplest adornments in the duet of reunion ('Parigi, o cara') whose headlong cabaletta ('Gran Dio! Morir sì giovine') discharges accumulated feeling.

What if the men's arias earlier in the work are not quite on the same level? Like Bellini's *Norma*, which inspires some of its music, *Traviata* belongs to the heroine. With a true singing actress it distils pure feeling, and is indestructible.

By its successful 1854 revival Verdi was in Paris, part way through the two-year stint that finally produced *Les Vêpres siciliennes* in June 1855. Ever since *Jérusalem* in 1847 he had wanted to write a five-act grand opera, complete with elevating historical theme and ballet. He rescinded one contract with the Opéra in 1849; he signed another in February 1852. By then a coup d'état had made Napoleon III the autocratic ruler of France. The new order was not Verdi's reason for going back to Paris, though in 1856, when more opera business took him there, the parvenu emperor and empress had the former democrat turned realist to stay for a week. What did at once move Verdi and throw up obstacles in his way was the need to compete with Meyerbeer, whose *Le prophète* was the portent of 1849, while in the 1850s his *L'Africaine* loomed in the offing, never quite ready.

It was also what led Verdi to insist on a full five acts; the veteran librettist Eugène Scribe, long dominant in Paris but now past his best, could not avoid stretches where the action treads water. The Opéra threw up its usual quota of difficulties; as an extra, the prima donna,

Sophie Cruvelli, vanished from rehearsals for a month in late 1854 with the opera still unfinished (she turned out to have gone on an unofficial honeymoon). Verdi fumed, tried to rescind his contract, got Scribe to draft and redraft, complained of indiscipline at rehearsals. *Vêpres* in the end had only fair success, and little more in Italy, where it circulated as *Giovanna de Guzman* with its locale shifted to Portugal (because the original showed an Italian revolt against an occupying power). After the 1860s it largely vanished. Revivals in our own time have left its standing doubtful.

The trouble is the requirements of Paris grand opera, a spectacular genre dependent on the cheap labour of chorus singers, dancers, extras, seamstresses, scene painters, scene shifters. Verdi did his best to fasten on intimate exchanges, but he could not ignore those requirements. Today not even the most highly subsidised theatre can afford to produce *Vêpres* on the original lavish scale; a performance shorn of spectacle disappoints. Verdi, besides, was to pin down all too accurately the result of opera-making by committee: with much fine music (praised by Berlioz) and some excellent numbers *Vêpres* remains a 'mosaic'. Its composer was to solve the problem of grand opera sixteen years later.

In Italy Verdi's position was now unique; yet once his Paris business was over – losing his action against the pirate manager of the Italian opera house, and putting on the French version of *Trovatore* at the Opéra – he felt he had to go back to his accustomed work rate, with contracts for two operas in 1857 and another for Naples in early 1858. It also meant going back to the accustomed stomach pains.

The Italian opera world had recovered from economic crisis. Verdi's favourite producer Lanari had, however, died in 1852; he still would not work with Merelli; like many others, he was to find the leading impresarios of the moment, the brothers Luciano and Ercole Marzi, unreliable when they put on both his 1857 works, *Simon Boccanegra* and *Aroldo* (the reworked *Stiffelio*). He took care to distance himself by making the contract for *Boccanegra* with the owners of La

Fenice, but the problem of the harum-scarum, at times literally fly-by-night impresario was to get worse and lead Verdi to make a decisive change.

Boccanegra shows what Verdi's drive for 'originality' could entail. When he looked at it again twenty-three years later he had to agree that it was a 'rickety table' whose legs needed adjusting (VB, 13); he revised it in detail and added a new climactic scene, but did not quite cure the limp. The trouble was not the music: a 1995 London concert performance of the original under Mark Elder showed a downright, powerful score that needs no excuse. The Spanish drama Verdi chose, by the ultimate author of *Trovatore*, deals in complex family relationships among people spread over three generations (one of whom never appears; two more reappear under aliases after a twenty-year gap) and the still more complex politics of medieval Genoa; because of the short-cuts unavoidable in a libretto, the audience to this day cannot tell why Amelia has been kidnapped and then freed – a crucial episode – or what moves the various patrician and plebeian factions. *Trovatore*'s wild plot does not matter: the emotional relationships are always clear. *Boccanegra*'s remains at once sombre and baffling. This cut short its nineteenth-century career. Today it is almost a favourite, in part because audiences now like problem works, in part because the obscurities fail to blot out some magnificent episodes. A problem work it remains none the less.

After the scant success of *Aroldo* five months later, it looked as though Verdi had followed his three most popular works with three that fully met neither French nor Italian taste. He next produced an opera that united French and Italian qualities, won lasting fame, and stands out among his works as uniquely exhilarating. Before it could establish itself, though, *Un ballo in maschera* put Verdi through his worst trouble with the censorship of the despotic Italian states – themselves about to vanish.

Since his first stay in Paris in 1847–49 Verdi had gradually taken over some of the language of French opera: in his Italian works from *La battaglia di Legnano* (1849) the old double-aria unit had at times

12 Verdi rehearsing *Simon Boccanegra* in Naples, 1858, with the poodle Loulou in attendance. Caricature by Melchiorre Delfico

given way to *couplets* (strophic songs with the melody repeated) or ternary numbers (in three contrasting sections, with some dramatic movement); he had learnt to orchestrate in more varied, more delicate colours. In *Ballo* he went further: he gave an Italian opera the elegance and dash characteristic of French music, allied to an intensity French opera seldom achieved.

This venture, it seems, had been maturing in his creative unconscious – perhaps a reaction from the stark *Boccanegra*: when he finally discarded *Lear* as a possible opera for Naples he got its librettist, Somma, to adapt the text Scribe had written in 1833 for a Paris opera, Auber's *Gustave III*. This, though technically 'grand', had piquant situations that lent themselves to treatment in part comic.

The subject was bound to cause trouble: a plot to assassinate not just a king but an historic figure of a couple of generations back, Gustavus III of Sweden, shot in 1792 at his own masked ball. Verdi was prepared to compromise as he had over *Rigoletto*. He and Somma quickly fell in with most of the censor's initial demands: a ruling duke for a king, no politics, no consummated adultery, no firearms; they still tried to smuggle in a period (the seventeenth century) that would justify a brilliant court life. Their effort turned out not to be enough, for a real subversive – an Italian – had meanwhile thrown a bomb at Napoleon III. The censor now made fresh demands: no ruler; no friend's wife for him to be in love with; no period later than the Middle Ages; no drawing of lots to choose the assassin; no ball; no masks; no onstage murder. The management got its own writer to travesty the libretto on these lines, setting it in medieval republican Florence.

Verdi held out. Naples, he said, had inflicted the 'customary monstrosities' on *Rigoletto*, but in his absence; he would not put up with them in an opera he had specially composed for the city and was to see through to the first night. His chief objection was to the new setting, hopelessly at odds with music written to fit an 'elegant and chivalrous' court. He withdrew the opera and set about arranging its production a year later in Rome – a snook cocked at the Naples authorities, for Rome was both near and little less obscurantist.

When the Naples management sued him (they presently settled out of court) Verdi listed his grievances with a flourish. Out of Somma's 884 lines, the proposed new libretto had altered 297; it had cut and added many more:

> I ask further whether the management's drama has in common with mine
>
>   The title? – No.
>   The poet? – No.
>   The period? – No.
>   The place? – No.
>   The characters? – No.
>   The situations? – No.
>   The drawing of lots? – No.
>   The ball? – No.
>
> A maestro who respects his art and himself neither could nor should dishonour himself by accepting, as the text for music written to quite another programme, these grotesqueries that violate the clearest principles of dramatic art and degrade an artist's conscience.
>
> (CV, I, 269–70; C, 565–72)[11]

Verdi appeased the Rome censor by shifting the action to seventeenth-century Boston, for Italian audiences a near-mythical place where, as absolute governor, an Earl of Warwick might well hold a brilliant court.[12] The Rome impresario, Vincenzo Jacovacci – famously mean because inured to a low subsidy – gave no trouble but for engaging some poor women singers; when he later tried to give *Ballo* at a reduced fee Verdi suggested that he should help himself *gratis* to the works of the long dead Lully, Gluck, and Paisiello.

Ballo's French inspiration shows in its five leading characters, one an adolescent page sung by a light soprano to whom Verdi gave three delicious, quicksilver numbers – a figure quite unlike the old Italian contralto hero; in the stretta of the opening scene, a virtual cancan by

Offenbach and just as irresistible; chiefly in a constant play of light and shade, passion and laughter, embodied in musical structures often cut down from their routine form and in translucent instrumental textures.

The outer acts have many fine things, in particular buoyant, unorthodox ensembles – the quintet 'È scherzo od è follia', making light (in all senses) of a present danger, the earlier trio 'Della città all'occaso' – Amelia's prayer riding above in noble concision – the ritual drawing of lots with pianissimo trumpet brooding high up, the concise trio-into-quintet that closes the scene; also the eloquent long line and innovative form of the baritone's aria 'Eri tu', and the *Don Giovanni*-like dance music, its suavity an ironic, tense-making comment on the impending murder. What seals *Ballo*'s quality, though, is the middle act – together with Act 3 of *Aida* the finest Verdi ever wrote.

Scribe contributed a chain of highly theatrical situations: Amelia's fearful errand under the gallows-tree; Riccardo's bursting in; her reluctant avowal of love; her husband's hurrying on to warn the ruler and his veiled lady that the conspirators have spotted them and are bent on murder; Riccardo's entrusting the veiled one's safety to his friend while he makes his escape; the conspirators' attempt to remove her veil – which she does anyhow to save her husband's life; jeers, despair, fury, deadly resolve.

All this was meat and drink to Verdi. Yet, as Harold Powers has shown, it is the music that shapes the act and controls its mercurial temper: what hits us is not 'opera as drama' but 'drama as opera'.[13]

For Amelia's tormented aria Verdi wanted 'something all in a turmoil [. . .] fire [. . .] agitation [. . .] disorder'; he made Somma rewrite in helter-skelter anapaestic metre.[14] 'Ma dall'arido stelo divulsa' rushes through despondency and resolve to a horrific vision overcome by prayer, its form a variation and then a shorthand restatement of the opening stanza, all held together by the cor anglais and the orchestra, its effect at once pathetic and headlong, crowned by the noble line of the prayer. The ensuing duet is the most lucent expression in opera of the deep mutual love of man and woman, something rare in Verdi and matched – at far greater length – only by *Tristan und Isolde*. The orchestra takes over at crucial moments; after Riccardo's urgent plea it broadens out, time appears to stand still, the cellos sustain the lovers' broken, ever more ecstatic exchanges (in unorthodox fashion they sing not together but answering each other), and their inner ecstasy returns to interrupt the cabaletta's outer, syllabically quick joy: as Verdi later wrote, there 'love had to burst out' (C, 642).

With news of the conspirators the trio ('Odi tu come fremono cupi') sets up irony within urgency: husband and wife sing together, yet he does not know whose stabbing high notes crown their driving plea to Riccardo to go. At the fall of the veil comes an extraordinary change: the leading conspirators Samuel and Tom greet it with an impudent little tune; this 'suddenly bouncy music [...] contrast[s] in every way with the portentous preparation [...] the unexpected abandonment of the key so elaborately prepared makes the affective gap between frightful and comical even greater' (Powers). Of the concluding ensemble Verdi himself wrote: 'the irony of [Samuel and Tom], the gaiety of the chorus, the wife's despair, the husband's fury formed a magnificent musical tableau'.[15] So they do. At curtain fall the audience should tingle with many-layered delight such as only opera – this opera – can give.

Soon after *Ballo* opened on 17 February 1859 war broke out between Piedmont, supported by France, and Austria. Within a few months Milan, Florence, and Verdi's own Parma (though not Venice) would join the as yet unofficial kingdom of northern Italy; so, within another year, would the whole of the centre and south (but not Rome and its immediate surroundings). This great change in the life of the country went together with a fundamental change in Verdi's working life. Thanks to copyright, the operas were now making money year in year out; the 'galley slavery' was over; the people's composer could afford to relax. If he wrote in future it would be at a time and place of his own choosing.

13 Verdi at the time of *Il trovatore*, probably of the French version (1857) since he is wearing the French Legion of Honour

5 Complications, 1859–1872: *La forza del destino, Don Carlos,* and *Aida*

With Italy independent and united, Verdi – one might suppose – felt happier about his place in the world and in the art of music. Not at all.

True, he and Strepponi greeted the coming of the new nation with unmixed joy; in the tumultuous years 1859–61 he joined – somewhat reluctantly – in the political processes that set up the new kingdom. Within a couple more years, however, Verdi entered a notably sour period in both his personal and his professional life. It was to last from his fiftieth year (1862–63) to about his sixty-fifth (1877–78); the mid-life crisis that hits some men in their early forties – or 'male menopause' – reached him late.

Till then his uncommon native energy had driven him forward: he took longer than most to hit a snag. The crisis, however, came also of developments in the new Italy that challenged his expectations and his standing as an artist. He came to feel disappointed with his country and bitter about changes in its artistic life that might have left him stranded. At Sant'Agata, where he now spent much time improving his lands, he had to cope with first an Italian, then a Europe-wide economic crisis, later still with the beginnings of trade unionism. One of his few deep friendships went badly wrong; as it deteriorated he became involved with a woman singer and caused a prolonged crisis in his marriage.

In these years Verdi often snarled at those about him and at the world in general. During his blackest phase the most trivial matters could set him jumping down his wife's and the servants' throats: 'I don't know' – Strepponi, at her wits' end, noted in 1867 – 'with what words and in what tone of voice I am to speak to him, so as not to offend him!' (WalkerV, 401). When he pronounced on Italian musical life Verdi took up the attitude he was never to move away from, of a thoroughgoing conservative nationalist. Yet these were years in which he composed three of his most notable operas and the Requiem; whatever else we may think, these works are innovative, they contain passages of a grieving nobility and beauty hardly matched anywhere, and one of the operas, Aida – written in the depths of the personal crisis – is as fully achieved as anything Verdi undertook.

The short, bloody war of Italian independence in which France joined Piedmont against Austria (April–June 1859) skirted Sant'Agata without breaking in. Verdi wrote that but for his lack of stamina he would have volunteered; gratitude to Napoleon III made him willing to put up with the 'blague [humbug] of the French, their insolent *politesse*, and their contempt for all that is not French' (C, 578). Almost at once, though, Napoleon's decision to end the war without conquering Venice or its territory plunged Verdi into despair: no reliance could be placed in foreign help. His seesawing reactions were typical of Italian middle-class liberals. He remained in fundamental sympathy with France as the wellhead of 'liberty' – political and, especially, religious – and of 'civilisation': during the Franco-Prussian war of 1870 he thought Italy should have repaid the debt contracted in 1859 and sent men to fight. Yet he grew hostile to France when it acted against supposed Italian interests, as in 1881 when it beat Italy to a protectorate over Tunisia (C, 604, 608–9).

What fixed Verdi in this bourgeois liberal attitude was meeting Cavour. In September 1859 the Piedmontese statesman had just united most of northern Italy by bringing off that rare feat, a political revolution that was socially conservative, but he had resigned over Napoleon's armistice. At that confused time Parma and its neighbouring region were not yet legally annexed to Piedmont. Verdi, drafted as one of the representatives sent to plead for annexation, met

Cavour at his country house; 'the Prometheus of our nationality' impressed him deeply (C, 582). From then on Cavour's brand of liberalism was to be Verdi's bible: strong for parliamentary freedom and economic improvement but on a narrow franchise and with an austere, authoritarian bent.

In 1861 Cavour, back in office, persuaded the reluctant Verdi to stand for the Chamber of Deputies that would proclaim Italy a kingdom united in law as – Venice and Rome apart – it was in fact. Verdi's prestige, Cavour argued, would help to counter 'extravagant opinions, adventurous ideas, revolutionary talk' and to keep in order 'over-imaginative' deputies from the newly annexed south (C, 588–9). The unspoken hint was that Verdi, a former democrat, still an anticlerical, would do something to offset Garibaldi, a democrat and an anticlerical then at the height of his fame as the liberator of southern Italy. In 1860, after Garibaldi's daring southern expedition with 1,000 volunteers, Verdi would have gone on his knees to him; in 1862 he supported the hero's doomed attempt to seize Rome, something he thought the king himself should have undertaken: 'oh Rome, Rome! . . . when will that day arrive! The dream of twenty years of life.'[1] By 1864, however, the Verdis had cooled towards both Garibaldi and his fellow-democrat Mazzini. Constant agitation had put them off; prudence was now in order.

Shortly after persuading Verdi to stand in 1861 Cavour died, to the composer's deep grief. He felt bound to let himself be elected, took part in the crucial vote on the kingdom of Italy (with Rome its hypothetical capital), but then was mainly abroad during the next two years; afterwards he was in the provisional capital, Turin, on and off. He claimed to have more than once tried to resign a post for which he had 'neither inclination nor aptitude nor talent' (A, II, 619), and he did retire at the next election.

His years as deputy had done little more than confirm his standing. This was now high both at home and abroad, whatever critics might say against his music. With it came the penalties of success in a Europe inching towards the mass society we know. Such penalties were to grow until in two months of 1880 Verdi's postbag brought forty requests for autographs or money or occasional compositions such as hymns. Already in 1862 he was astonished during a stay in London to find that unknown people wrote in for autographs and some enclosed a self-addressed envelope.

Verdi put up a stout resistance both to time-wasting requests and to honours clumsily offered. Some of this was the 'bearishness' he liked to claim, some a proper sense of his own worth: on being asked in 1864 to join a musical committee which the superannuated Pacini would chair, he commented 'with my respectable self as doorkeeper perhaps' (A, II, 798). His life from then on would, all the same, be lived in the public eye, represented by newspaper gossip rather than, as today, by visual media; no paparazzi hung around Sant'Agata.

His chief business abroad in 1861–62 was the pursuit of French grand opera by other means. After the three 'popular' works and *Un ballo* Verdi no longer need prove himself as a composer of Italian opera, but he still lacked an unmixed success in Paris. Achieving it was clearly the supreme challenge, for all his complaints about the 'big shop'. In these years the Opéra was taken up chiefly with laborious preparations for Meyerbeer's *L'Africaine* (at length given in 1865); Verdi knew there was no room for him. When the Russian imperial opera at St Petersburg offered the chance of a lavish production with first-rank singers at a record fee of 60,000 francs (£2,400), Verdi seized the opportunity; he wrote an epic work on the Paris model, with ambitious crowd scenes and touches of French comic as well as grand opera, but to Italian words by the faithful Piave, whose last new Verdian libretto this was to be.

Like Shakespeare's *Macbeth* in the British theatre, *La forza del destino* is known in Italy as the unlucky opera. Verdi experienced its 'evil eye' when the prima donna fell ill and the whole production had to be put off from January to November 1862. For him and Strepponi this meant two winter journeys to Russia; on their first return trip they nearly froze (and their stock of wine did) in an unheated railway carriage on the 120-mile stretch through Lithuania. As he launched a second production in Madrid Verdi began to feel dissatisfied with a drama he had originally called 'powerful, singular, and huge' (A, 11, 634). He had himself dictated words, metres, whole scenes, but – as with *Boccanegra* – had based them on one more wild Spanish play, rambling across time and space and ending in a pile-up of violent deaths. He kept toying with changes; in 1869 he gave the battle and duel scenes a new order and some new matter, ended the tragedy on a note of austere Christian resignation, and launched it again in Milan, incidentally making peace with La Scala now that Merelli was no longer in charge. *Forza* went into eclipse late in the century; like *Boccanegra* it has come back in our own time, yet it remains a problem work.

The problem is not its epic looseness, which suits modern taste, so much as its eye cocked towards Paris. Verdi thought the 'vast tableaux' were 'the real musical drama' (C, 619), yet the gipsy Preziosilla and the soldiers, peasants, and muleteers with their choruses and dances too often hover on the edge of Second Empire frippery, nowhere more than in the Rataplan, where the massed forces imitate a fife and drum band. *Forza*'s best 'tableaux', so to say, are in Musorgsky's *Boris Godunov*, a work which it influenced.

The heart of Verdi's opera dwells in Leonora's aria 'Madre, pietosa vergine' and in the duets, especially those between her and the abbot of the monastery she flees to and between the two male leads, one of whom has vowed eternal vengeance on the other. Generous souls hounded by fate draw from Verdi 'that halo of sorrowing greatness with which he crowns the loser, the outcast, and the defeated'.[2] It works through melodies of a line characteristically noble, above all at the climax of Leonora's aria (already heard in the overture, where the rushing 'fate' theme pursues it as it does the heroine throughout): a soaring and then further soaring arch (it spans a ninth) recalls those described by the earlier Leonora of *Trovatore*, now seared by experience. Such patterns do something to unify the work and set its *tinta*, but it remains an opera of great moments.

The Italian opera world into which Forza was loosed after St Petersburg and Madrid could not now afford a Verdi first performance: his three operas of 1862–71 were all launched abroad. Not only had Verdi priced himself out; the genre was entering a period of artistic crisis. Since about 1845 repertory opera had grown and with it the number of large theatres catering for a mainly shopkeeping and artisan audience; even subsidised theatres gave fewer new works. Verdi's successes of the 1850s had masked the failure of other composers to strike home.

About 1860 a group of young poets and musicians known as the 'dishevelled ones' launched a campaign for renewal. As often in such movements, a good deal was generational assault and mutual puffery, but the *scapigliati* brought in aestheticising French influences (Baudelaire and Gautier) and out-Hugo'd Hugo in pursuit of the violent and the grotesque. In music they joined a wider group who discovered German instrumental works and, in the 1860s, launched 'quartet societies' to perform them (not necessarily confined to chamber music). They admired Meyerbeer; 'the music of the future' was as yet a slogan loosely attached to Wagner (none of whose work Italy would hear before 1871), but whatever it might be they would create it.

To such a group an established artist of Verdi's standing was a lion in the path – who might yet turn benign. Relations were at first warily cordial. The twenty-year-old Arrigo Boito wrote the words of a 'Hymn of the Nations' which, for once, Verdi set – an occasional work for a London exhibition that committed neither man deeply; the twenty-three-year-old Franco Faccio hoped Verdi would approve his first opera. Alas, he did so in late 1863 just as Boito recited a poem calling on 'young Italian art' to escape from 'the old and cretinous'; Faccio, he hinted, would 'raise modest, pure art on the altar now befouled like the wall of a brothel' (A, II, 762). Who had fouled the altar of Italian music if not the leading composer of the day?

Verdi was understandably wounded, and stayed wounded. Sixteen years later, when he and Faccio were not merely reconciled but close collaborators, he still brought up 'fouling the altar' in a letter.[3] Meanwhile, in 1865, he wrote sarcastically to the like-minded Piave (with an allusion to a windy article of Boito's in praise of 'spherical' art):

> These so-called apostles of the future have started something great and sublime. It was necessary to *cleanse the altar befouled* by the swine of the past. We need pure, virginal art, *holy, spherical!!* I look up and wait for the star that will show where the Messiah has been born, so that I, like the Magi, may go and worship him. *Hosanna in excelsis*, &c. (A, II, 825)

In his reaction he turned against 'classical' music and those members of quartet societies who pretended to enjoy it: most of it meant 'being bored to death' (A, II, 778, 800). He in effect made his publisher Ricordi give up sponsoring the quartet society's journal. Later, as Italians' interest in symphonic music deepened, these grumbles of 1864 would swell into a litany of complaint: to Verdi's mind, a wilful, anti-national fashion was drawing the country's music out of its true path.

It made no difference that he himself borrowed scenic effects from Meyerbeer and instrumental ones from several foreign composers, that the man who was to write in 1879 'instrumental music is not our art' (C, 525) clothed all his mature operas in skilled, often delicate orchestral writing undreamt of in the traditional Italian genre, or that while denouncing quartet societies he was to compose, at an idle moment in 1873, a delightful string quartet; true, he presented it as a diversion, took three years to publish it, and did not follow academic sonata form, but this highly individual piece showed a far deeper, more masterful engagement with harmony and counterpoint than had earlier Italian quartets like Donizetti's, written for friends to play among themselves. Verdi, we may guess, genuinely thought foreign models dangerous for Italian composers – other than himself: consciously or not, he acted as if he alone had the power to integrate them into a style unmistakably Italian.

What helped to make Verdi more and more conservative in all things other than his own work was his new status as a well-off landowner. In the 1850s and 1860s he was rebuilding and adding to the house at Sant'Agata; even when composing in Paris or elsewhere, or wintering in Genoa, he sought to control the running of house, garden, and estate by post.

'I mean to be master in my own house', he wrote to his steward in 1867: the garden must be shut up and the house servants told not to go out of it on pain of dismissal – all but the coachman, who was to exercise the horses every other day, though he too must be watched; in later years servants who went out in the evening had to be back by 10 p.m. The 1867 steward was himself unsatisfactory: 'you will never learn either to *command* or to *obey*!!' (C, 547–51). Soon afterwards Verdi took on as factotum at Sant'Agata a former impresario, Mauro Corticelli: him too he instructed 'Let no one else be master, trust nobody,' yet at the same time told him off for interfering in the steward's business: 'I am absolutely resolved to put everyone in his place and make everything run well.'[4] Verdi, a natural autocrat, demanded that anyone who took his place should both exact total obedience from others and show it to him – a combination not easily secured outside a Prussian army regiment.

True, an improving landlord such as Verdi had his work cut out. While he was abroad for much of 1862–63 the then steward turned embezzler; the building works set in train came to a halt. After a quarter-century's experience Verdi wrote that the harvest was poor because 'the peasants are always stubborn'; so they would be until a way was found to give them 'a little schooling' and to improve their condition (C, 551–2). Yet he seems never to have thought of building them a school. He did build them a cottage hospital – rather late, in the 1880s, after he had witnessed a man with a broken leg being taken by oxcart to Piacenza some twenty miles away and yelling at the bumps on the road. Perhaps the only likely schoolteacher would have been a priest: it was one thing to employ nuns as hospital nurses – Verdi criticised them for spending too long in church but defended them as

14 Verdi's house at Sant'Agata at an early stage of development. The original house has been added to but the trees have not had time to grow to full height. Contemporary engraving

having authority over their patients – quite another to take on a clerical teacher when, with the Church unreconciled to the new Italian state, the country priests would in any case 'end by subverting all the peasants' (*CV*, III, 30). Perhaps, again, the weight of illiteracy and custom seemed too great.

Verdi's answer was close supervision and discipline. When in residence he interviewed steward and tenants twice a week in the local dialect, taking notes; he attended cattle markets in neighbouring towns, feeling the animals to test the skin. While away he still went through accounts in minute detail: why were some posts missing from a fence put up by one of the tenants? The steward must report which cows or mares were pregnant, when their offspring were born, and what price they were fetching at market; the horses must be fed Sant'Agata hay and their manure fully used.

In the early years he would not take on married servants: 'that makes two enemies, always in collusion against the master'. In 1881 he sacked a father and son for insubordination, over the pleas of his lawyer and friend Angiolo Carrara, whose son had by then married the Verdis' adopted daughter: 'in a countryside like ours the more you do [for people] the worse you are served: and I who could live like a gentleman in any capital city, respected by all, spend my fortune and waste my time in one of the ugliest places in Italy, among people who show neither gratitude nor respect'. He threatened to leave Sant'Agata for good. Verdi as landlord was the type of the peasant turned master, fit for a novel by Balzac.

He was not alone. In the late nineteenth century many men of plebeian origin took over and improved the lands of the plain south of the Po. By the time Verdi had built up his estate through repeated purchases – the largest in 1870 and 1875 – he owned (in 1891) some 1,613 acres, a good slice of the area between Parma and Piacenza. On some of it he built or rebuilt tenants' houses; his tenancy contracts enforced mixed farming (of cereals and cattle) and modern crop rotations, including, from 1875, clover or other legumes to keep up fertility, as well as cheese making and the upkeep of roads, ditches, buildings, and insurance, all strictly at tenants' expense. To irrigate his lands he acquired in 1867 a steam pumping engine from London, costing £265 and weighing five and half tonnes; to control the local river he bought more farms; to avoid floods he built up the bank along the Po. He read agricultural manuals, was interested in marling (the use of clay as fertiliser), and made a modest start with the new chemical fertilisers.

Unfortunately he bought much of his land just before agriculture entered a prolonged slump. His rent roll, about 22,800 francs (£912) a year in 1867, may not have totalled much more a quarter-century later, when the estate was much larger but some tenants had fallen into arrears; at the worst of the crisis in the early 1890s he lowered the rents, though he insisted on being paid the lowered rents (and the arrears) in full.

The trouble was the coming of cheap food from the Americas and Australasia, and then a trade war with France; depression set in from 1873 and hit bottom in 1879–93. Even in the late 1860s the grist tax with which the new state loaded its fast rising debt interest on the poor meant – Verdi was aware – that landless peasants were 'starving to death'; by 1878 he was writing to his parliamentary ex-colleague and friend Giuseppe Piroli that the government met poor people's call for work and bread with 'soldiers and handcuffs': at that rate workers and peasants would one day 'turn the world upside down'. This did not mean that he was in sympathy with farm labourers in 1882 when they struck in a nearby village, demanding a ban on threshing machines and a share of the harvest. He wanted the government to act against 'agitators', thought himself safe from them, but once again threatened that if they reached his farms he would leave (CV, III, 50, 134, 139, 155–6).

As with international affairs, Verdi reacted to each new event in turn, generally by foreseeing the worst: neither industrialisation (just beginning in the 1880s) nor emigration (in full swing throughout his time at Sant'Agata) would help Italy. His abiding preference was for the honesty and 'firmness' shown by Cavour and his immediate successors of the liberal Right – those who had brought in the grist tax.

At Sant'Agata Verdi sometimes described himself to acquaintances as 'peasant, bricklayer, carpenter, porter', 'architect, master builder, smith', someone who ran about 'all day from house to the fields, from the fields to the house'. At other times he spoke of a quieter routine: up at 5 a.m. to shoot quail, look in on the builders after breakfast, then an hour or two's nap, followed by household business and letter writing, then dinner, a walk until dark, a gossip over cards, and to bed (VI, 259; C, 546–7).[5] His daily round no doubt varied with the intensity of the works he had set in train. He is unlikely to have done much physical work himself – not in a period of superabundant cheap labour, when he employed sixteen men and two women on the garden alone, up to six of them full time; in the kitchen, which produced excellent meals, he now and then cooked a fine risotto. In any case he was at Sant'Agata for only about half the year.

His own view of himself as landowner shows in the house and garden which he and Strepponi built up – both preserved little changed. The house, though they added to it, claims no aristocratic status; the rooms are of middling size and height, easily kept warm in winter, the furniture solid and elaborate in the Italian variant of mid-Victorian style, the pictures for the most part anecdotal or of personal interest. The garden, again of middling size for a villa, adds more trees and a pond to the few oaks already there in 1848; magnolia grandiflora, willows, cedars, further oaks make a shaded oasis in the plain, though the Verdis were old by the time they could enjoy their new trees at full height. It is a gentleman farmer's house, with far more books and music than such a person might normally collect.

The gentleman farmer and his wife lived much alone. The pattern had been set in 1849–51 by the ostracism the unmarried Strepponi met in Busseto. She never forgave it: 'to think', she told Verdi in 1853, 'that that lofty soul of yours came spontaneously to lodge in the body of a Bussetano!'. Marriage in 1859 came too late to help. 'A single family near us would suffice to break the monotony of [our] existence,' she wrote in 1861; she meant a family unlike those actually in the neighbourhood, whom four years later she called 'these cretins' (WalkerV, 213, 246, 251).

True, about 1860 tensions with Verdi's older relatives eased. From 1861 he let his ailing father occupy the Busseto town house. Carlo Verdi shared it with his aged sister and two servants; his little great-niece Filomena Maria Verdi too lived with them though her parents occupied Carlo's old house at Roncole – an arrangement not unusual at the time. With Verdi's other 'father' Antonio Barezzi and his second wife relations were good. Both father figures died in 1867; the Verdis, we have seen, mourned for both, though more intensely for Barezzi. They also decided to help Filomena Maria, then aged seven; by the following year they set about adopting her. Maria (as they called her) spent much of the next few years at boarding school; for the rest she was to live with them at Sant'Agata as their daughter and, in 1878, to be married from the house. For Verdi the marriage meant a closer link with the bridegroom's family, the Carraras; it also brought an heir.

With the remainder of Busseto things went badly. The cause was the gossip inevitable in a tiny town with a great man living nearby. Verdi treated it as an extension of the early to-do over Strepponi; in 1871 he denounced his fellow-townsmen for having put about or tolerated 'disgraceful slander' over the previous twenty years (C, 246–7). Their failure to appoint his disciple Muzio as music teacher rankled; the clerical party – both Verdis knew – still ruled. The building of a theatre in Busseto further soured relations.

To Verdi the theatre was a pointless extravagance. A group in the Busseto town council, however, wanted to capitalise on their native son by naming it after him; very early in his career, they recalled, he had privately undertaken to write an inaugural opera. From their small-town perspective they could not see that Verdi had outgrown them; when it came to the point he surely would deliver. Public statements implying as much brought Verdi crashing down in reproof, first in 1845, then in 1865 when the theatre was near completion. He was furious at a seeming attempt to force his hand, all the more because he had heard local people bring up the scholarship the town had given him, totalling 1,200 francs over four years: 'we made him!'. He offered to repay the money; as to moral obligation, 'I hold my head high and say with pride "Gentlemen, I have carried your name with honour to the ends of the earth. That is well worth 1,200 francs!'" (C, 14–15, 433–7). After much to-do he and the council patched it up; in lieu of an opera he contributed 10,000 francs; he cut off for a time his brother-in-law Giovannino Barezzi, guilty of 'crying out against me in the public squares'. The affair, Verdi wrote ten years later, left him 'a kind of pariah' in his home town (VI, 183).

Guests at Sant'Agata were accordingly few. Some came from the opera world – Piave and one or two others from Venice; later, members of the Ricordi family from Milan. The factotum Corticelli, it seems, was taken on in part as a jester with a supply of theatre gossip, but one more literate than the run of theatre people: he could draft letters in French. Verdi, however, was right in calling him a muddler. Worse, in 1879 Corticelli embezzled the savings of two women servants and had to be dismissed. He then tried and failed to drown himself in the canal at Milan; Verdi for a time allowed him 100 francs a month. Altogether it is not surprising that the tomb at Sant'Agata for which Verdi wrote the epitaph 'To the memory of one of my most faithful friends' should be that of the beloved poodle Loulou, who died in 1862 after a few years with the Verdis. A mastiff called Black lived somewhat longer; other, bad-tempered dogs followed.

One guest from the opera world who started coming to Sant'Agata in the late 1850s, the conductor Angelo Mariani, and another who made her first visit in 1871, the soprano Teresa Stolz, figured at the heart of the most dispiriting episode in Verdi's life.

In Italian opera Mariani was a portent: a leader of the orchestra who became the first conductor of the modern type and, in his day, the best. He was eight years younger than Verdi, hence just over thirty in 1852 when, as conductor of the Genoa orchestra, he showed that an Italian could meet the demands of Meyerbeer's Paris operas, thought at the time to be the last word. He and Verdi met on and off from 1846; they became close friends in 1857, when they worked together on the first performance of *Aroldo*. Mariani often came to Sant'Agata, where he had an open invitation; he wrote frequent, garrulous letters; he let Verdi and Strepponi heap commissions on him – find rifles for volunteers in the 1859 war, exchange a shotgun, send thirty yards of lace, procure autographs of famous people for Verdi's growing collection, order a statue or ten magnolia trees, five feet tall, and see to the exceedingly awkward business of shipping them by rail. He became Verdi's willing slave.[6]

Unhappily – as Frank Walker's definitive account of the relationship brings out – Mariani was a thorough neurotic with a masochistic bent. He grovelled to Verdi; answered some reproof with a string of '*Mea culpa*'s; addressed the man he 'venerated' and 'adored' four times in nine days to excuse likely shortcomings in the Genoa production of *Un ballo* – which then turned out a great success. His idea of a thank-you note after a stay at Sant'Agata was 'I would give ten litres of my blood to be beside you with my gun.' At the same time he had an awesome capacity to dither, to prolong his indecision, and to involve his friends in it. Repeated occasions for dither were the handsome offers that came his way. He could neither bring himself to turn them down (on the reasonable grounds that his Genoa appointment carried a pension) nor to leave Genoa and strike out as a freelance; when, in 1863, he was tempted by an offer from the Italian opera house in Paris, Verdi gave him excellent practical advice, but he dithered till the offer lapsed. He was, finally, good-looking, vain, untruthful, and sexually inconstant.

A touchstone is Verdi's lifelong disciple Emanuele Muzio. He too was loyal beyond question; yet his letters (to third parties) suggest that within this discipleship he coped with his master in straightforward fashion – that his 'yes' was 'yes' and his 'no' 'no'. Muzio himself cast a cool eye on Verdi's touchiness: 'Bear in mind', he warned Tito Ricordi, 'that men of genius torment themselves and torment still more those who deal with them!' (A, II, 346). How far Verdi tormented Muzio we do not know: probably less than he did Mariani, whose neurosis seems to have fed not only into Verdi's bullying strain but into a malicious vein in Strepponi. At first Verdi called Mariani 'Wrong Head' and treated him as an irresponsible boy, no worse; Strepponi laughed at 'that great babbler and provoker of babbling'.

The three of them became more closely involved in 1866: Mariani took great trouble to lease on the Verdis' behalf two floors of the Palazzo Sauli-Pallavicino in Genoa – owned by Marchesa Pallavicino, with whose daughter he may have had an affair – so that his friends could winter in a grand apartment with a terrace overlooking the sea; he himself took part of the attic floor on a sub-lease from Verdi. He could now worship his idol from aloft.

In March 1867 he and a newcomer, the dramatic soprano Teresa Stolz, both went to Paris to attend the first performance of Verdi's *Don Carlos*. Stolz, then thirty-three, had trained in Prague, capital of her native Bohemia; after early experience in theatres around the Black Sea she had launched a successful Italian career. Photographs suggest a blonde grenadier, letters suggest an unremarkable person with limited professional concerns (money, complacency, jealousy), but her voice and acting, together with some emanation that eludes us, were to capture both Mariani and Verdi.

In autumn 1867 she sang Elisabeth at Bologna in the Italian first performance of *Don Carlos*; as conductor Mariani showed 'genius'. Another kind of genius led him to find excuse after excuse for not meeting his Genoa commitments; to his friends' irritation, he tried to explain the delay by the need to tend 'Verdi's glory'. Probably at this time, he and Stolz became lovers – officially 'engaged' the following spring; they did think of marrying, but Stolz's career may have stood in the way. Mariani's health, too, was giving trouble – perhaps already from the bladder cancer that was to be misdiagnosed in 1870, and to kill him three years later.

With Verdi and his wife Stolz became well acquainted when she sang Leonora in the revised *Forza del destino* at Milan in February 1869; she had met Verdi some months before. Strepponi at first declined to come to rehearsals; from Genoa, three weeks before the first night, she wrote Verdi a bleak letter in which she accused him of wanting to slip her into Milan at night 'like a bundle of contraband goods' and described herself as having been 'repudiated'. Just what provoked this we do not know, though she mentioned harsh words and silences like those she had recorded in her diary a few months earlier. At that time

15 The conductor Angelo Mariani

she had brooded over her decision to give over her life to Verdi: 'Wouldn't it be right for him to say that he is satisfied with that, *at least* once a year!?' Now Verdi came to fetch her and she went to the Milan *Forza* after all. He may not yet have been infatuated with Stolz, as he clearly was to be three years later; or he may not have admitted his own feelings to himself.

16 Verdi's disciple and only student Emanuele Muzio

What – besides unconscious jealousy – tipped Verdi into outright war on Mariani was his own plan for a memorial requiem mass to Rossini, with leading Italian composers contributing a section each, to be performed at Bologna in November 1869 on the first anniversary of Rossini's death. He had thought it up in every detail, none of which must be changed; this largely explains why the mass was not performed until 1988.

Mariani, himself involved in other Rossinian celebrations at Pesaro, offered to help; Verdi threw his offers back in his face: 'Do you mean to say that we've got to entreat you, in order to obtain the chorus you have at Pesaro? [. . .] I have never been able to discover whether the project [. . .] has had the good fortune to be approved by you.' Mariani, he implied strongly, had acted out of 'the vanity of the composer or the arrogance of the performer' and had placed his own need for flattery and adulation ahead of 'something good, artistic, and patriotic'. Mariani's self-justifying reply was more dignified than usual; Verdi ignored it. He later claimed that Mariani had failed to answer; denounced him to Ricordi and others as having 'failed in his duty as a friend and an artist'; and silently took over the plan for an amateur chorus which, when Mariani had proposed it, he had swept aside.

The resulting breach was uneasily made up early in 1870. By July Mariani was undergoing severe pain from the cancer; he went, in hope of a cure, on pilgrimage to the shrine of the Virgin at Loreto and shamefacedly told the anticlerical Verdi about it. Strepponi had earlier dismissed his ills as 'fables no one believes'; she now drafted a letter for Corticelli – equally hostile – to sign, denouncing Mariani as a 'hypocrite' who out of 'measureless vanity' acted the part of a 'vulgar bigot' and inflicted it on Verdi. Because he had passed on a normal request from a soprano, Isabella Galletti, to be considered for the opera Verdi was then writing, the letter implied at length that he was a disreputable womaniser. How Verdi, Strepponi, and Corticelli worked themselves up into the poisonous hatred evident in this letter is unclear. Corticelli no doubt saw Mariani as the rival court jester, Verdi harboured another, perhaps latent rivalry, but Strepponi? Exasperation built up over years, and living in solitude where resentment could fester, may account for their behaviour – though scarcely excuse it.

The final episode turned on who should conduct the first performance of Verdi's new opera, *Aida*, in Cairo, and who should sing the title part there or, soon afterwards, in Milan. The Franco-Prussian war held up the launch for a year: the sets and costumes were in Paris, under siege. All the arrangements therefore had to be made afresh for the new date, often with new artists.

In November 1870 Mariani, regardless of Corticelli's onslaught three months earlier, offered himself as conductor; Verdi replied 'If I had thought fit to send you [. . .] I should have asked you.' He added more insulting hints about Mariani's supposed affair with Galletti. At that point he wanted Muzio to conduct. In April 1871 Verdi probably imposed the casting of Stolz as the Milan Aida in spite of her stiff financial demands; she and Mariani had dickered for Cairo, but the new date clashed with her other engagements. Muzio, meanwhile, also turned out to be unavailable for Cairo. Verdi fell back on Mariani – an unflattering second choice. Mariani's neurosis led him first to accept, then to dither, then to dither some more, finally to miss an appointment with Verdi. '*Trop fort!* [that puts the lid on it!] *trop fort! trop fort!*' Verdi wrote. Though Mariani was constitutionally unable to cut his losses – he went on sending third parties endless, pathetic letters about his unrequited love for the Verdis – the friendship was at an end.

In September and October 1871 Stolz spent three weeks at Sant'Agata. Immediately afterwards she broke off her engagement to Mariani: they would just be friends. He, meanwhile, was at Bologna rehearsing the first Wagner opera to be heard in Italy, *Lohengrin*; its first night on 1 November was seen by many as epoch-making. Because Ricordi's chief competitor Lucca was promoting it the whole Verdi–Ricordi camp treated Mariani's share as a betrayal. Verdi attended a performance; during an interval Ricordi's agent provoked a quarter-hour demonstration in his favour that rattled the cast and orchestra. Earlier that day Verdi had run into Mariani at the station; he had declined Mariani's offer to carry his bag and had cut the conversation short. They never met again.

In early 1872 the Verdis and Mariani, now ill with severe intestinal spasms and haemorrhages, were in the Genoa palazzo, avoiding each other; Mariani heard rumours that Stolz and Verdi were having an affair. That spring and summer Stolz too rounded on him: to Verdi she wrote sarcastically about her former lover's 'humbug'. Strepponi for her part drew up a catalogue of Mariani's 'filthy' behaviour. Late that year Verdi decided to evict Mariani from his Genoa quarters if need be – he had indirectly suggested his leaving – but then chose not to renew his own lease: the Pallavicinos were raising the rent, something the Verdis interpreted as Mariani's revenge. Verdi was to find other splendid winter quarters in the Palazzo Doria.

Mariani died in June 1873 after months of ghastly suffering made worse by wrong or missing care which one cannot help suspecting his own unconscious need brought down on him. Over the previous eighteen months the Verdis had at length acknowledged that he was ill, though on the eve of his death Strepponi was still writing venomously about him and the Pallavicinos as 'a complex of dear persons worthy of associating and understanding each other'; Verdi, she said, had greeted Marchesa Pallavicino's attempt to make peace between 'the two old friends' with an exclamation of disgust.

In our own time friends may quarrel and say appalling things which the telephone or now e-mail leave mercifully unrecorded. Nineteenth-century people wrote down ill-feeling for us to gawp at. Something must be allowed for this when we look over Verdi's dealings with Mariani. Then too, Mariani was his own executioner. That said, the story leaves a bad taste. It was far worse than the type of quarrel common in the hard-pressed Italian opera world of 1839 where Verdi had made his debut – a brush fire soon over; it was blown upon, tended, raked up, banked down. This could happen first because Verdi now had leisure to brood, secondly because his usual need to have those about him do his will grew, in these years, specially intransigent.

Did Verdi and Stolz have an affair? Probably – a continuing one – though they covered their tracks and no plain answer emerges. What matters is that Verdi fell head over heels in love with Stolz. To us she seems ordinary: Verdi, we may infer, projected onto her what a Jungian would call his anima – his feminine aspect – so thoroughly as to endow her with every lovable trait. His few known letters to her say little but often speak of his 'joy' and 'happiness'. Stolz for her part probably fell in love with Verdi, though it may have been difficult to tell love apart from gratification at having a genius love and admire her

17 Verdi at the time of *Aida*, 1872. Bust by Vincenzo Gemito. Several versions exist; this one is at Sant'Agata

and further her career. She wrote fuller letters but often addressed them to both husband and wife; even those we know addressed to Verdi alone were formal and worded so that Strepponi could read them without upset.

Verdi's sexual relationship with Strepponi had very likely petered out – perhaps not long after they were married in 1859. Late in the following year she wrote to him 'I hold you close, as in the *active* period of our life' (A, II, 595). Strepponi's mature letters are full of calculated hints; what this one hints at seems clear. She was then forty-five, had had chaotic sexual experience in early youth, and may well have lost interest while remaining wholeheartedly attached to Verdi and emotionally dependent on him. In the early 1860s she was also beginning to suffer from painful 'stomach cramps' – heralds of many internal troubles over the next thirty-odd years – and to put on weight. Sexual frustration in Verdi – we can imagine but not document it – may have helped to set off the rages over trifles that so alarmed his wife.

By spring 1872 she had something else to worry about – his attachment to Teresa Stolz. With Stolz singing *Aida* at La Scala Verdi not only supervised the production, he took an intense interest in the singer's business affairs and even her property jewels; against habit, he kept going to Milan to catch later performances. When he was not there, Stolz wrote to him; Strepponi docketed one lot (in pencil) 'Sixteen letters!! in a short time!! what *activity*!' Stolz also made frequent visits to Sant'Agata. The three of them then spent the period from November 1872 to April 1873 in Naples, again for an *Aida* which Verdi supervised. Rumours flew; Strepponi afterwards tried to challenge Stolz (still singing in Naples) by having a friend ask her whether she had heard 'this infamous tittle-tattle', but the friend could not bring himself to do it.

As in the previous year, Strepponi fell into depression. To her and Verdi's old friend Clarina Maffei she wrote 'A grey veil has fallen over my spirit and I no longer believe in anything' – not even in God.[7] From the start she had kept up the tactic of writing Stolz friendly letters peppered with hints – 'I like to be sure that when I shake your hand I shake the hand of a sincere and loyal woman, who loves me a little.' When, in 1875, the three of them went to Paris and London for performances of Verdi's Requiem Mass, with Stolz in the soprano part she had created, Strepponi put up with something like a *ménage à trois*: they stayed at the same hotel and had their meals together in the Verdis' suite. A scurrilous article in an Italian magazine heavily hinted at an affair; Verdi, it said, had lost his wallet in Stolz's hotel room. The trio skated over this

18 Giuseppina Strepponi in her sixties

too; at most Stolz asked whether she might not be in the way at Sant'Agata and Strepponi reassured her.

In spring 1876 all three went to Paris again for *Aida*, with Stolz in the title part. Some three weeks into their stay Verdi insisted on visiting Stolz alone – she had been slightly unwell but was not ill, and there was no performance that night to worry about. In these circumstances Strepponi drafted a protest against his pay[ing] a call on a lady who is neither your daughter, nor your sister, nor your wife! [. . .] you could spend twenty-four hours without seeing the said lady [. . .] since 1872 there have been periods of assiduity and attentions on your part that no woman could interpret in a more favourable sense [. . .] I have always been disposed to love her frankly and sincerely.

You know how you have repaid me! With harsh, violent, biting words! You can't control yourself. [. . .]

If there's anything in it . . . let's get this over. Be frank and say so, without making me suffer the humiliation of this excessive deference of yours.

If there's nothing in it . . . Be more calm in your attentions, be natural and less exclusive. Think sometimes that I, your wife, despising past rumours, am living at this very moment *à trois*, and that I have the right to ask, if not for your caresses, at least for your consideration. Is that too much?[8]

Whether Strepponi passed on this letter we do not know. Back in Italy the 'attentions' went on through the summer. Verdi made more flying visits to Milan; in August he may have met Stolz at a tiny spa not far from Busseto.

In September Stolz spent several weeks at Sant'Agata. In October Strepponi began a draft letter 'Since fate has willed that that which was my whole happiness in life should now be irreparably lost [. . .]'. There was a showdown – which we know nothing about for sure; according to hearsay – from a credible source – Strepponi declared 'Either this woman leaves the house, or I leave it,' and Verdi replied 'This woman stays, or I blow my brains out.' Strepponi won – outwardly: Stolz, though she had just announced her retirement, went off to sing in Russia for six months; from then on her letters were far fewer, and she did not again visit Sant'Agata for two years, by which time she had retired for good. After that she made regular visits, and joined the Verdis on trips to Paris and to the spa at Montecatini where they spent the early summer, but whatever her and Verdi's relationship amounted to its conduct was now discreet.

Was Strepponi content? She never stopped admiring Verdi and loving him 'with a crazy affection'. In 1878 she showed her mastery of the calculated hint by giving him her photograph inscribed 'To my Verdi, with my former affection and veneration!' With Stolz she established a sisterly relationship, though here too she dropped the occasional hint: at Christmas 1876, right after the showdown, she mentioned the Christian duty to forgive the offender; two years later her New Year's wish for Stolz was 'every good thing [. . .] that an honest person can desire'.

Yet she may have settled for keeping up appearances. One more draft letter to Verdi (which she may not have sent) perhaps dated from 1880. In it she suggested wintering no longer in Genoa but in Milan, where Verdi could have more social life; though she did not say so, Stolz lived in Milan. 'I ask only for an apartment with light and air, and that you do not abandon me completely in these last years of life.' Nothing came of this. Verdi was to give up Genoa for Milan, but in his own very last years, after his wife's death in 1897. Consistent to the end, Strepponi left Stolz some jewels in her will. By then Verdi was very old. At eighty-seven he wrote to Stolz, then sixty-six: 'Believe in my [love], great, very, very great, and very true.'[9]

It says much for Verdi's autonomous creative gift that he could write *Don Carlos* and then *Aida* amid this turmoil. He also had to swallow what he thought the disgrace of the 1866 war in which Italy obtained Venice and its territory not as a conquest (it had failed on both land and sea) but as a gift from Napoleon III.

Don Carlos mounted a last direct assault on the Paris Opéra: in five sprawling acts taken from Schiller; on a pseudo-historical subject, the struggle between liberty and clerical oppression at the court of Philip II of Spain; with seven principals and a ballet (now hardly ever performed). Some think it Verdi's finest opera, though it too remains a problem work.

The problem, as with *Les Vêpres siciliennes*, is that of French grand opera – in 1867 a genre about to disappear. Verdi went back to 'the big shop' in part because he was at length allowed a flat fee of 40,000 francs (£1,600) on top of royalties, in part because he still wished to outdo Meyerbeer. He himself complained two years later of 'that fatal atmosphere of the Opéra': it had made Rossini's *William Tell* less spontaneous than his *Barber of Seville*, and turned every grand opera into a 'mosaic' (C, 220–1).

Such is the mosaic of *Don Carlos* that Verdi needed to rearrange it. He shaped three main versions, in 1867, 1884, and 1886, with wide differences. In 1884, for the sake of 'concision' and 'sinew' (C, 698), he cut out a whole act; in 1886 he put it back again; both times his style, a good deal altered since 1867, made some passages condensed and harmonically bold far beyond the rest. He had also made deep cuts before the original first night – to keep the length down, perhaps on artistic grounds as well – and further important changes in 1872. As scholars have retrieved the material cut in 1867 a production now puts together its own mosaic from a wide range of sources, all at one time sanctioned by Verdi. Italian operas often had alternative versions of a scene or aria, but the variations in *Don Carlos* were chameleon-like.

That said, *Don Carlos* is the masterpiece of French grand opera. The heroic stature of its characters, all justified by their own lights, their emotional depth, the sense of generous feeling wrecked on the asperities of power make it – one critic maintains – actually 'too short [...] in proportion to its rich dramatic substance'.[10] Yet few would deny that it 'feels its length'.[11]

If all dwelt on the height of the last two acts reservations would vanish. Before Philip II's aria 'Elle ne m'aime pas' 'the heavy acciaccatura sobs on horns, bassoons, and strings convey that iron grief which lies at the heart not only of Philip but of the opera as a whole'; weary solo cello and obsessive muted violins join them to sound the depths of the authoritarian yet noble king.[12] As in his queen's parallel aria at the start of Act 5 ('Toi qui sus le néant') Verdi works the French ternary aria form and his own mastery of instrumental writing into a Hamlet-like soliloquy, each high-souled character caught in a personal and political tangle to be loosed only in death, yet still vibrant with love, tinged with aspiration or regret. Less amply (because the character has been less developed) he does it again in Princess Eboli's aria of repentance and resolve ('O don fatal'). Already in 1867 he brings to full bloom the showing forth by voice and orchestra of a human predicament that had begun in Lady Macbeth's sleepwalking scene twenty years earlier.

The formidable duet in which the grand inquisitor, aged and blind, demands of the king the head of the libertarian Posa marks a giant step towards free dialogue in music. From trombones, bassoons, and lower strings a theme that uncurls like a heavy snake sees the inquisitor on and off; in between the orchestra flexibly, sparingly comments on the dialectic between church and state. By contrast the scene for the imprisoned Carlos and his bosom friend Posa, ending in the friend's murder and death, used in Britain to be thought sentimental, like their Act 2 duet of brotherly love ('Dieu, tu semas dans nos âmes'), which comes back here in reminiscence; perhaps because we have become less frightened of emotion, they now seem straightforward and right, though Posa remains a two-dimensional figure best served by Verdi's earlier style. Posa's Act 4 romanza ('C'est mon jour suprême') 'transform[s] into gently expressive music the dark, tired motive that began the scene [...] the force of human communication has briefly overcome the force of destiny'.[13] His dying song ('Ah, je meurs'), like the Act 2 duet, works as a slow cabaletta bringing emotional release.

The remainder of Acts 4 and 5, much improved in 1884, includes the last of the three duets between Carlos and his stepmother and lost love Elisabeth, all of them beautiful, innovatory, and dramatically right. The awkwardness of *Don Carlos* lies in the uncertain proportions of the whole, also in such Parisian byways as Eboli's scarf song and the exchange of masks. A rambling mansion, but noble and mighty.

Both in Paris and in Italy *Don Carlos* had only fair success. Verdi, it appears, went on feeling the need to settle accounts with grand opera. He would do it away from Paris and its 'fatal atmosphere', would rely on the Italian language he knew best, but would otherwise meet the demands of the genre once and for all.

He still relied on Paris for a subject: in 1868–69 his friend Camille Du Locle, one of the two librettists of *Don Carlos*, kept sending him plays in both French and Spanish, none of which Verdi liked. In the end Du Locle forwarded a scenario by another Frenchman, Auguste Mariette, an archaeologist employed by the khedive (viceroy) of Egypt. This was part of the khedive's effort to celebrate the opening of the Suez Canal; he had tried in vain for an ode or, later, a new opera by Verdi to launch his new theatre (aimed chiefly at European tourists); his officials went on trying. This time Verdi thought Mariette's plot well made, the setting magnificent, one or two of the dramatic encounters 'very fine' though not quite new: 'Now let us consider the financial situation in Egypt and then we'll decide' (CV, IV, 9).

'The financial situation' had a lot to do with the making of *Aida*. Verdi demanded and got an unprecedented 150,000 francs (£6,000) for the Cairo production alone; the singers treated it as a bonanza. They joined those Europeans who since the mid 1850s had flocked to Egypt, about 30,000 of them a year, and those others – mainly French and British – who had bought Egyptian government bonds or Suez Canal shares. As a producer of fine cotton, strategically placed on the route to India, the country saw – and its rulers encouraged – an investment boom of a kind we are familiar with, for instance in Indonesia under General Suharto. Investment was often misplaced even when it did not go to pay for high living by the ruler and his friends. The result – in 1876, five years after *Aida* – was the country's bankruptcy, leading after six more years to a British protectorate.

Though *Aida* did not mark the opening of the canal, its launch in Cairo was a minor incident in European imperial expansion. Did Verdi own Egyptian bonds, like the anti-imperialist prime minister W. E. Gladstone (who none the less was to sanction the bombardment of Alexandria)? Perhaps; the bonds were standard fare on the Paris market.[14] We should, however, be mistaken if we concluded, like many people in the wake of Edward Said, that *Aida* is itself a document of 'orientalism' – the imperial appropriation of a misunderstood culture.

In 1870, when Verdi wrote *Aida*, Italians engaged hardly at all in European expansion save as migrant labour; it was all they could do to pick up Rome while the Pope's French garrison were away fighting Prussia. When, in the 1890s, Italy did join the scramble for Africa, Verdi opposed it: the Ethiopians 'will not know what to make of [our "civilisation"], and in many respects they are more civilised than we!'; British rule in India too would one day face a 'Risorgimento' (IEV, 351). While writing *Aida* he showed little concern with modern Egypt as other than a patron.

Ancient Egypt – 'a civilisation I have never been able to admire' (A, III, 161–2) – did stir him to inquire about ritual and especially about musical instruments. When an opera subject invited local colour Verdi asked for music of the time or place; he then as a rule disregarded what he found. Here too the trumpets in the triumphal march are ancient but not Egyptian, the priestess's chant modal and remote-sounding but invented, the exoticism subtle, lightly touched in. The story uses Egypt as a pretext: archaeologist or no, Mariette took many liberties. It does not help *Aida* that the audience looks for arena spectacle, quadriga on the go, ostrich fans aloft. The plot goes back to classical tragedy; its many intimate scenes gain when they are freed from the aura of the British Museum.

Nor has *Aida* to do with imperialism except in the most generic sense. True, authority wins: to avoid underwriting it producers now show absurdities like the triumphal march without a march on stage, or the Egyptians as British occupiers in pith helmets, or the Ethiopians as downtrodden blacks. In fact *Aida* could be set in any warm climate where an autocratic, priest-ridden state fights a simpler hill people: ancient India, modern Burma, Tsarist Russia in the Caucasus, pre-1914 Turkey in its Slav domains. The tale of the soldier and his enemy's daughter, both torn between love and patriotism, is timeless; so, by definition, is the Aida–Radames–Amneris triangle.

Verdi wrote much of the libretto himself – unofficially. With Piave disabled by a stroke, he used a competent writer, Antonio Ghislanzoni, to tidy up the structure, the metre, and, often, the actual words he laid down. Climactic moments, he insisted, called for 'theatrical words' (*parola scenica*) that bore an unmistakable meaning; he imposed a number of them, such as, in Aida's duet with her father, 'You are not my daughter, you are the Pharaohs' slave!'. 'I know' – he told Ghislanzoni –

> you will ask: what about the verse, the rhyme, the stanza? I don't know what to answer; but when the action demands it, I would at once give up scansion, rhyme, and stanza; I would write irregular verse so as to express quite clearly all that the action requires. In the theatre, unfortunately, poets and composers must now and then have talent enough to write neither poetry nor music. (C, 641)

Verdi had not always been thus single-minded. For *Trovatore* he had set the words of 'D'amor sull'ali rosee' to pre-existing music, here and there ignoring their normal stresses. The demand for *parola scenica* signalled a move towards greater realism, as did Amneris's denunciation of the priests after the trial of Radames – 'one of those intensely concentrated musical periods which in mature Verdi does duty for a whole aria'.[15]

Aida is indestructible because it sounds a great range of drama by the pithiest means. Grand opera was inconsequential, mastodontic; *Aida* secures grandeur within tight, logical action and only two and a half hours of music – in a triumphal scene as brilliant as the *auto da fé* act in *Don Carlos* but less flashy; in ballets short and integral to the action, each a cornucopia of tunes; in marches aptly four-square ('Su, del Nilo') or at once archaic and catchy (the famous one at the height of the triumph); and in a chorus ('Ma tu, re') where the priests demanding death and the people begging for clemency work the apotheosis of the traditional first-half finale, at once a piece of complex musical architecture and a satisfying embodiment of dramatic conflict.

At the same time an intimate tragedy works itself out among four people, all characterised in their music even if they miss the overliterary complexity of Philip II and Don Carlos. Amonasro's fierce authority and Amneris's expansive, wilful persona come out the moment they open their mouths; Aida's nature, generous yet wistful, informs her orchestral motive before she comes on, while her outburst ('Ritorna vincitor!') at the end of the first scene shows her capacity for high feeling, with its concluding anti-cabaletta 'Numi, pietà' an index of her purity (if Verdi by April 1871 had fallen in love with Stolz, no wonder he wanted her to sing the part). About Radames the opening scene tells all, in the subdued fanfares at his hopes of command and in the gently accompanied romanza 'Celeste Aida', its culminating high B flat (given the right singer) a limpid sunburst, never stentorian. (Verdi cannot have expected tenors to sing it pianissimo as marked; this, like his occasional marking *pppp*, tried to shock musicians out of bad habits.)

The glories of *Aida* are its orchestration and its 'string of duets'. Flute and high, muted, dancing strings at the start of Act 3 effortlessly call up a still, warm night beside water; later, thoughts of the Ethiopian hills bring instrumental writing of astringent delicacy. Throughout the work 'the *Aida* style' shows an unobtrusive mastery: 'regular and periodic, with swift and unpredictable changes of harmony [. . .] and chromatic inflexions that caress without cloying'.[16]

The duets carry the emotional action: Aida's moment of truth as Amneris smokes her out in Act 2; her collapse before Amonasro and, immediately afterwards, her entrapment of Radames in Act 3; Amneris's vain attempt to save and win back Radames in Act 4. As earlier in *Rigoletto* and *Traviata*, they are built in dovetailed sections, with a new concision and flexibility; so too are Aida's 'Ritorna vincitor!' and her elegiac Act 3 aria 'O patria mia'. Again one cannot do better than send readers to Petrobelli's title essay in *Music in the Theater*. Verdi, he demonstrates, in Act 3 shapes the structure of both words and music so that they fit with and determine each other and, by setting the length of each section, propel the drama: that gift rare in opera, full control of musical–dramatic time, comes to urgent bloom.

Add the originality, beauty, and aptness of one melody after another – the consolatory long line of 'Rivedrai le foreste imbalsamate' and 'Là, tra foreste vergini', Amonasro's vision of slaughter, the

19 Why Verdi admired the production values at the Paris Opéra: Aida, Act 3, 1880. Contemporary engraving

martial ardour of Radames's 'Nel fiero anelito', many more; add too the simplicity of the final duet as the entombed lovers send their arching melody soaring twelve times in an ecstasy of grace while, above, Amneris prays for the peace of Radames's soul – an effect at once impressively theatrical and intimately moving, all of it Verdi's own work – and it becomes clear that *Aida* signals his final mastery.

After Cairo and Milan in the winter of 1871–72, and two more Italian productions supervised by the composer, *Aida* went all over the world. Verdi, nearly sixty, thought he could retire with his ambitions fulfilled.

6 Evergreen, 1872–1901: the Requiem, *Otello*, and *Falstaff*

By the Milan *Aida* of 1872 Verdi stood at an angle to the Italian opera world. His prestige in his own country was unmatched, yet his last three operas had all been written for theatres abroad. Even when they were to be given in Italy he no longer dealt with local impresarios: all correspondence now went through Ricordi. Verdi's relation with his publisher governed the last twenty-five years of his creative life: the third-generation head of the firm, Giulio Ricordi, flattered and nursed him into creating, against his declared wish, two extraordinary late blooms of Italian opera, *Otello* and *Falstaff*.

Since the early 1850s music publishers had gradually taken a hold on the Italian opera business unexampled elsewhere. As the old aristocratic theatres and their attendant impresarios weakened, publishers used the leverage the new copyright gave them to decide which theatres should perform an opera and when, and who should sing in it; by the 1870s this was normal practice. With the score and parts of each opera, publishers sent out uniform designs for scenery and costumes as well as – a novelty learnt from Paris – elaborate stage directions. A publisher's office in Milan ostensibly controlled 'its' works throughout the Italian opera business, which now took in lucrative outposts like Argentina. In practice it could dictate casting; in minor theatres, nearly everything else as well.

Two publishers, each enlarged by a series of mergers, battled it out during the rest of Verdi's career. The firm of Lucca had been the first to make a new opera into a package deal; after the death in 1872 of the tactless Francesco Lucca his widow Giovannina Lucca ran the business with verve and a common touch. This doughty woman and Verdi might have got on; by then, however, she was committed not just to Meyerbeer and other Paris composers but to Wagner, while Ricordi stuck largely to Verdi and other Italians. This meant war between the two firms, directed not just at capturing important seasons but at running down each other's products – until in 1888 the ageing Lucca sold out to Ricordi, which thereby acquired Wagner's works and, overnight, discovered their merits. A new threat appeared at once – Edoardo Sonzogno, who owned the rights in *Carmen* and promoted young Italians like Mascagni. For several years late in the century Ricordi and Sonzogno in turn ran La Scala. Ricordi's period of control meant that an Italian opera house could once again afford the original production of a Verdi work.

Verdi's dealings with his publisher, we have seen, could be stormy when he thought he had been ill treated. With time, his operas became ever more clearly the firm's mainstay; this gave him great bargaining power, yet he needed Ricordi's distribution network and its control of local managements. Tito Ricordi, head of the firm from 1853 to 1888, still an old-fashioned tradesman in outlook, was his near contemporary; the intimate 'tu' terms they were on did not preclude some harsh disputes. Tito's son Giulio, who from the 1870s took over much of the non-financial business, was, in contrast, a flower of the new Italian bourgeoisie: fashionably dressed (while Verdi went on with the baggy suits, artist's flowing bow tie, and broad-brimmed hat of the 1850s), close to the aestheticising younger generation of writers and artists, himself a minor composer, he addressed Verdi in the elaborate polite form. Like Disraeli with Queen Victoria, he laid on flattery with a trowel.

Flattery was needed to smooth over what Verdi took to be slights. Like other publishers and agents, Ricordi put out a music journal, largely to promote its own artists and run down the opposition. Verdi reasonably expected it to promote him too; he was, though, ultra-sensitive to what struck him as less than wholehearted praise. Already in

20 Giulio Ricordi, shown as the quintessence of fin-de-siècle aestheticising Italian culture, a strong contrast to Verdi's earlier, earthier Italy

1845 he had complained to the founder, Tito's father Giovanni, that the paper as a rule carried 'now an article *in my defence* that's worse than a criticism, now a comment that's almost an insult etc. etc.': should he count Giovanni 'among my enemies or my friends'? In 1855 he wrote that the paper had spoken ill of him for three or four years. As late as 1879 he took a saying of Rossini's, reported in the journal – that he,

Verdi, would never manage a comic opera – as a warning from the firm against any such attempt; if he did try, he concluded, 'I shall ruin some other publisher! . . .' (A, I, 541; CV, I, 32, IV, 94; C, 308–11). More complaints, and discreet warnings from Strepponi, came from time to time.

Verdi none the less claimed that he had never sent Tito Ricordi or any other owner of a journal 'a single word of complaint [. . .] it doesn't fit in with my habits or my character'; 'I never complain, even about hostile articles' (A, II, 445, III, 256). He no doubt meant that he had often felt like complaining but had checked himself. Like many successful artists, Verdi kept his thin skin.

After *Aida* he had grounds for complaint, not against Ricordi but against critical opinion. The opera, he knew, was one of his best or, as he put it, 'least bad' (VI, 140–1). It still met incomprehension. Throughout Europe and America controversy raged over 'Wagnerism', a term then little understood; in Italy the war between Ricordi and Lucca sharpened it further. Because Verdi's style had evolved towards more flexible forms and subtler instrumentation, critics detected the influence of Wagner. They were to repeat this cliché until, at Verdi's death thirty years later, Shaw declared 'without reserve that there is no evidence in any bar of *Aida* or the two later operas that Verdi ever heard a note of Wagner's music'.[1] Verdi had – without taking much from it. *Aida*'s recurrent musical tags were unlike the Wagnerian leitmotiv with its psychological development; they fined down a device, the 'reminiscence theme', that Verdi had tried out clumsily in *I due Foscari* twenty-seven years earlier, and to better effect in *Traviata*.

Amid the chatter about 'Wagnerism' even the best-informed Italian reviewer saw an awkward shift from the 'modern' parts of the score – fed by international influences – to the 'old-fashioned' cabaletta of the Aida–Radames duet. Not for the last time, Verdi mocked at the conventionality that had once doted on cabalettas and now put them under a ban: 'Oh! What a flock of sheep!!' What mattered was that a cabaletta should be effective in its place. He remained embittered at 'stupid criticism, and even more stupid praise [. . .] with at bottom a sort of peevishness, as if I had committed a crime in writing *Aida* and having it well performed [. . .] No one has even said to me: *Thank you, dog!*' (VI, 144; A, III, 553).

Verdi got round critical opinion by himself seeing the first Italian productions of *Aida* onto the stage; Wagnerism or no, the work carried all before it. This meant spending time and energy, first in Milan, then in Parma and Naples to get his way over both the musical performance and the production. The experience took up all of 1872 and the early months of 1873. It deepened the irony with which Verdi regarded La Scala ('the first theatre in the world' according to the Milanese); at the San Carlo, Naples – beset with 'ignorance, inertia, apathy, disorder, wreckage' – people still complacently assumed that 'we' knew best, just as officials of the Paris Opéra went on about their monopoly of 'taste': 'nous, nous, nous' (A, III, 445; C, 276, 280, 683–7). To get his new work across, Verdi saw, he would have to take full charge, battling routine mediocrity all the way – and he did.

Over *Aida* – and, earlier, over the revised 1869 *Forza* – Verdi acted as a producer in the modern sense; till then he had essentially coached the singers. Like Wagner at Bayreuth a few years later, he accepted the 'historical', realistic scenery and costumes then in vogue; true, he disliked clutter and seems to have hankered after the less 'rationalistic' style of the 1840s. His innovations, he had told Tito Ricordi apropos of *Forza*, were simple: that singers should 'learn to read and understand' their parts, impresarios to produce, orchestras and choruses to keep together and observe piano and forte markings: 'It's as though a painter asked for a bit of light to let a picture be seen' (A, II, 733). By the 1860s the coming of repertory opera had let standards slip; many operas were put on at a singer's behest, with little or no rehearsal. These bad habits easily spread to new productions. 'For want of a stage manager' at Covent Garden – Shaw was to write in 1891 – 'no man in *Les Huguenots* knows whether he is a Catholic or a Protestant.'[2] Verdi's 'simple' innovations were to the point. In Italy he was to influence, among others, Arturo Toscanini (who as a young man worked with him) to make stagings in leading opera houses more coherent.

This meant adequate rehearsal time. For *Don Carlos*, in 1868 new to Milan, Verdi demanded (in vain) forty days against the Italian norm of three weeks. In 1883 he protested again, to marginally better effect, when singers in the new cut-down version looked like rehearsing for just over a fortnight. Italian orchestras, he found, needed to fill out their long neglected middle strings – violas and cellos – so as to make a more homogeneous sound; they should also overcome their habitual faults of 'violence and lack of delicacy'.[3] From singers he demanded, as always, 'fire, spirit, vigour, and enthusiasm', but this did not mean shouting or 'putting your hands to your head and going stark mad'.[4] We cannot hear the results: his active career ended just before records came in. He does seem to have allowed plenty of rubato; his insistence on performing the score 'exactly as written' was a warning against sloppiness rather than a literal demand.

As Verdi worked from 1869 in leading Italian theatres he was concerned at the dire state of the opera business. The Italian government had withdrawn from subsidy of theatre seasons or orchestras – now left to increasingly reluctant town councils; worse, it had imposed a 10 per cent tax on box-office takings. Verdi's next enterprise in 1873–75 came together with the onset of economic depression. Some of the theatres he had worked for as a young man – La Fenice in Venice and La Pergola in Florence – were now closed more often than not.

The parlous state of opera was not, however, Verdi's reason for launching in these years the Requiem Mass for Manzoni. He had retired from the lyric stage; writing a sacred work was, for an Italian composer, a normal next step. The mass stood in a long tradition; its layout was common form, with the Libera Me at the end carried over from the aborted 1869 mass for Rossini. Verdi had contemplated a requiem before Manzoni died on 22 May 1873, aged eighty-eight, but the event drove him into action which this time brought the performance of the mass a year later. He conducted it in a Milan church, then at La Scala, finally on tours to Paris and London and, later, to Vienna and to a festival at Cologne; Ricordi's cancellation of a performance in Berlin – because of low bookings at a depressed time – led to a furious dispute between composer and publisher over their whole relationship.

An Italian Scott, Dickens, and Tennyson rolled into one, Alessandro Manzoni was an austere Catholic as well as a moderate nationalist. Verdi had held him in awe since reading *The Betrothed* at sixteen. Only in 1868 did his friend Clarina Maffei take him to meet the frail old man she called her 'saint'; for the second time in his life he felt like kneeling to a human being (Garibaldi had occasioned the first). This genuine reverence apart, we need not suppose Verdi to have written the mass out of Christian feeling, though the form of Christianity uppermost in his day may have coloured its expression.

Like many nineteenth-century artists, Verdi was an agnostic whose elevated sense of morality and duty bypassed divine sanction. Strepponi, replying in 1871 to a friend bent on Verdi's conversion, at first wrote that, with the highest virtues, her husband was an atheist; she then revised this to 'I won't say an atheist, but certainly very little of a believer' (WalkerV, 280). We have no reason to doubt her. She herself was at that time a theist who, while distrusting organised religion, went to church; she gradually moved closer to orthodox Christian belief.

As he extended Sant'Agata in the 1860s Verdi built a chapel, but that was a measure of social discipline. Like other landlords, he made his subordinates go to mass; he disliked priests in general and the local incumbent in particular; like some other anticlericals, he made an exception for a favoured priest, Canon Giovanni Avanzi, an Italian patriot and incumbent of the next parish, Avanzi became a friend and officiated at Sant'Agata, for instance at the wedding of the Verdis' adopted daughter. When in residence, Verdi attended: it was a condition of having mass said in a private chapel. Only very late, about 1890, do we hear of his accompanying his wife to church in Genoa.

After its early performances the Manzoni Requiem had few until the 1930s; it is now one of the most popular of sacred works. The old

21 Verdi in his seventies

view of it as 'operatic' has waned; neither its forms nor its language come from opera. It may suit a post-Christian age because it now strikes Christians as dubious: to them – and a few others – it 'smells too much of sulphur'.[5] The prospect of hell appears to rule; the cataclysm unleashed by the Dies Irae not only dominates with its choral Niagara and offbeat strokes on the bass drum, it haunts the work in unliturgical reprises – two in the first half and another just before the end. Terror in the face of judgment does loom large in the medieval text, but another agnostic composer, Fauré, eight years later was to set a kindred text so as barely to touch on the Dies Irae in passing. His version is consolatory; Verdi's, troubled to the end, is not.

The nineteenth-century priests who taught Verdi probably instilled fear of hell as a central Christian attitude; compare the sermon in Joyce's *Portrait of the Artist as a Young Man*. About his late Te Deum of 1896 Verdi was to say that the lone utterance at the end – 'I have hoped in Thee' – was that of 'humankind fearful of hell', not the most obvious interpretation of the words (VB, 490). Verdi, we know, held a bleak view of life; if there was a next life it too might be something to dread.

That said, the Requiem balances high drama with dignity of utterance, power with translucent orchestral weaves; humankind troubled at the day of judgment holds the foreground, yet shafts of light come in – at the held-in collective grief of the Lacrymosa, the Hostias with its repeated inclined simplicity, above all the extraordinary Agnus Dei: the two women's voices in octaves three times unfold a plainchant-like melody that circles back on itself, stepwise, their variations of mode and key twined with shifting necklaces in the winds – prayer at its serenest. The dancing Sanctus, a breakneck double fugue, speaks from a unique artistic temper, and so does the anxious final fugue ('achieving salvation by violence' according to Francis Toye). What if the individual soul faced with the Other shows more clearly in Leonora's 'Madre, pietosa vergine', or the sense of collective prayer in 'La vergine degli angeli', both from *La forza del destino*? The Requiem is a public work, much of it grand, declamatory; it remains a great public occasion.

This, apparently Verdi's last work, confirmed him as the unique presiding genius of Italian music; talk of 'Wagnerism' came from an intellectual minority. No fellow-composer – not Ponchielli or Gomes or, a little later, Catalani – came near him in popularity or reputation; Puccini was to make a decisive mark just as Verdi retired in earnest. Such eminence was flattering but exposed.

Governments and other official bodies of united Italy held Verdi in high honour. In 1874, the year of the Requiem, he was made senator for life; not that he attended the upper house after his swearing in. Away from Parliament he spoke out on matters of artistic policy, chiefly in letters, some of them meant for publication. Ministers and officials asked him to sit on committees looking into musical education, to promote a statue to Bellini, to accept the honorary citizenship of Milan or Bologna, to comment on this and that – invitations he as a rule turned down, though he now and then gave way. The bigwigs, however, seldom took his advice.

His invariable stance was hatred of both advertisement and self-advertisement. He wanted nothing to do with the Bellini statue if it looked like promoting another statue to himself. He refused to attend productions of his own works he had had no hand in merely to show himself. It was, he wrote, 'deeply deplorable' that a leading Italian critic should travel to Cairo for the first night of *Aida* (C, 272). Even a newspaper report that scene and costume designs had been sent to him for approval made him 'feel ill' (VB 82–85, 155). The value of his own new operas, he said again and again, was best shown by the takings at the fifth or sixth performance. Nor would he express an opinion about other composers' works, old or new; this was canniness, and so was the pose of rustic ignorance that underwrote it.

In a country where modern journalism was starting up, Verdi declined to act like a public figure except now and then when it suited him. His insistence on privacy for the work he had in train fed speculation – in particular when he forbade for years any news of what he planned for the two late operas or how far he had got with them. Verdi, it seems, was not sure whether he would finish *Otello* and especially *Falstaff*; he also liked to tease. About *Otello*, which he had virtually finished: 'Shall I finish it? Perhaps! Shall I have it performed? Hard to tell, even for me!' (VI, 331–2). So shrewd a man of the theatre was not quite innocent of 'backing into the limelight'; nor did he object in principle to Ricordi's boosting in its journal both his operas and his charitable acts.

The new Italy, like the old, worked through a net of patronage. Verdi once told his friend Clarina Maffei that as an opponent of privilege he neither could nor would recommend anyone for a job, 'not even my best friend' (A, III, 453). This too must be taken with a pinch of salt. He did recommend people for jobs – even a priest, a friend of Canon Avanzi's, for a change of parish – and when he did his word would be taken; he in effect appointed the first head of the new music conservatory in his own city of Parma – Franco Faccio, who turned out to be mortally ill – and then his replacement. When, some years later, he recommended his coachman's son for admission to the conservatory and the ministerial bureaucrats ruled the boy out – he was just over the age limit – Verdi put on a burst of sarcasm:

> NO MAN IS A PROPHET IN HIS OWN COUNTRY...
> If I had been born a TURK I might have got what I asked!
> I none the less bow to the Minister's elevated wisdom.
> How happy we are! – Severely governed as we are, we shall turn into a nation of perfect beings.
> Excuse me and goodbye. (C, 404 (note))

The boy got in.

Nor was Verdi above getting friends in high places to ensure that on journeys to and from Paris his luggage was spared a tiresome examination by Italian or French customs; there would, he said, in any case be nothing dutiable. This use of privilege was common form, even if it did not quite fit Verdi's general attitude of Roman republican austerity.

On artistic policy for the new Italy Verdi made a theoretical case – that of a nationalistic old grouch. At the same time he made a practical case for changes in musical education and in the financing of opera companies and orchestras. This rested on his own long experience; some of his proposed changes came about – well after his death.

His theoretical case, endlessly repeated over four decades, was the one he had first made when stung by Boito's 1863 attack and the rise of quartet societies. Italian music was taking the wrong path because young composers were scared of what pundits would say and did not heed their own spontaneous impulses; in their fear and insincerity they aped foreign models – German symphonic music above all, but French as well – and sought rarefied harmonic effects that did not go to the heart. Instrumental or symphonic music was fine for Germans, wrong for Italians. The Italian genius was for vocal music; Italians should stick to that. True, Rossini had taken over 'some forms' of Mozart's, but he had remained a true Italian melodist:

> [. . .] that we should give up [our national characteristics] for the sake of fashion, out of a mania for novelty and an affectation of scholarship, that we should repudiate our own art, our own instinct, that craft of ours, spontaneous, natural, sensitive, dazzlingly luminous, is absurd and stupid. (A, IV, 78–9)

Musical education should therefore stick to Italian models, preferably old ones. In a formula of 1871 – it was meant for publication and quickly became famous – Verdi wrote 'Let us go back to the old: it will be a step forward' (C, 232–3). When asked, he would put forward a list of composers worth students' time and effort; this began with Palestrina – a fixed point – and went on with Carissimi and with eighteenth-century luminaries of the Neapolitan and Venetian schools, chiefly Alessandro Scarlatti, Marcello, and Pergolesi. Young people should not study modern music; they should spend little time on instrumental music of any period.

As so often, Verdi's inner feeling was more complex than the rigid line he laid down, and his practice in part went against it. Though he gave Pergolesi a high place in his syllabus, he privately assigned the composer's Stabat Mater to 'the *boring* genre', a genre it shared with much of J. S. Bach's output (VR 80–81, 22, 25). Again, though Verdi found the B minor Mass 'a bit arid' (VI, 320) he owned, on occasion played, and in some sense admired Bach's music. Besides picking up instrumental ideas from Beethoven, Berlioz, and Mendelssohn, he owned the scores of Wagner's operas down to *Parsifal*. His semi-official response to Wagner's death in 1882 ('Sad! Sad! Sad! [. . .] a

name that leaves a most powerful mark on the history of [our] art!!!',
VR 82–85, 86) did not fully show his considered opinion of the man's
work: he seems to have thought it uneven and long-winded, and yet
admired the sensuous expressiveness it won through bold harmonic
invention.

Verdi harped on the Italian vocal tradition in part because he felt
beleaguered, in part because the crisis in Italian music other than his
own did arise from a doubtful sense of identity. In the new, uncertainly
united Italy of 1860–1900 nationalist feeling combined dependence
on foreign models with effortful claims to superiority; Verdi, though
as a liberal wedded to the 'civilising' French example he disliked
Italy's alliance with Germany and Austria, went out of his way in 1889
to praise the blustering, aggressive prime minister Francesco Crispi,
chief upholder of the alliance. In music, before Mascagni's *Cavalleria
rusticana* of 1890 signalled the coming of the 'young school', Italian
composers did flounder, unable to integrate foreign influences with
native habits. A return to pure vocal music was scarcely practicable;
Verdi himself, we have seen, moved with bold innovative step into ever
subtler instrumentation while still giving the vocal line first place.

Even as he urged on conservatories a purely Italian syllabus, Verdi
cast doubt on the education they offered – as a former rejected candidate well might; what mattered was individual teaching and strong
leadership. He did, however, join others in wanting music students to
have a better general schooling, and girls to be admitted in places like
Naples where they were not. What he really cared about was the state
of opera: it was no use reforming conservatories if Italian theatres
were going to the dogs. The government, he urged, should repeal the
10 per cent tax on box-office takings and go back to subsidising at
least three leading opera houses, in Milan, Rome, and Naples. It
should put their orchestras and choruses on an annual salary; free
choral schools should turn out men and women bound for a time to
sing in the opera chorus – a system pioneered in eighteenth-century
Parma. Governments eventually did most of these things, but not till
the 1920s or even the 1960s.

22 Verdi's study in Sant'Agata

Verdi might have spent his sixties and seventies as a grouch, an artist fallen idle – but for an occasional psalm setting – after a glorious career, and more and more of a back number, if two men had not coaxed him back into the opera house. These were Giulio Ricordi and Arrigo Boito.

'I am here to obey you and carry out your wishes' (VR 82–85, 143). To call into being a new Verdi opera Giulio Ricordi made himself the composer's slave, like Mariani but with incomparably greater acumen and farsightedness; Verdi thrust on him such tasks as choosing a wedding present for the daughter of the Milan hotel manager in whose best suite he usually stayed.

Giulio's sustained attention was needed after the 1875 crisis in dealings between composer and publisher. Already upset over cuts and interpolations in performances of *Don Carlos* and over the cancellation of the Requiem in Berlin, Verdi found irregularities in the firm's accounts: he had not been paid all he was entitled to. The parties nearly went to law but, after complex negotiations, settled for a payment from Ricordi of 50,000 francs. Verdi later lent Ricordi 200,000 francs, needed in the parlous 1880s; this, in effect an investment in the firm, was still outstanding at his death.

Giulio spared nothing to keep the master in play. As well as hastening to meet Verdi's complaints and requests, he made the most of his genuine reverence for an artist he once playfully compared to God creating out of chaos. No other composer was worth anything: 'without you... we can't go on... and [our] theatres and [our] art will be ruined!' (VR 82–85, 58, 62). In 1879 he took the occasion of a Requiem performance which Verdi conducted in Milan – gratifyingly successful; Ricordi perhaps helped to marshal a cheering crowd under Verdi's windows. At dinner among friends Giulio suggested that Boito might write a libretto based on *Othello*. Verdi understood at once; when, however, Boito and his old friend Faccio called on him next day, and Boito three days later brought an outline libretto, Verdi would only encourage him to go on: the result would do 'for you, for me, for someone else'(C, 311). Boito presently delivered a full text;

Verdi bought it from him, but still would not commit himself to writing the opera. The seed had none the less been planted.

Of the 'dishevelled ones' who in 1863 had given Verdi such offence, Faccio had long since made amends; he had conducted *Aida* in Milan with what Verdi called 'rare, perhaps unique' skill,[6] and had launched it in Padua as the composer's deputy; he was to conduct *Otello* to general acclaim, only to founder in 1890 with tertiary syphilis. Boito, however, had met Verdi only once, by chance. He had made himself into a composer – of one opera, *Mefistofele*, a success in a tame revised version after initial scandal; of this 'music of the future' Verdi told a friend that it lacked 'spontaneity' and 'melodic invention', a withering bullseye (VI, 201). Boito had none the less made a name as poet and librettist and as a man of European culture. To Verdi he offered a command of literary scholarship and Italian metres as well as vast experience of writing words for music. Unfortunately, according to several modern Italian critics, these very advantages could turn into drawbacks: because he respected Boito as a literary man Verdi let him get away with precious wording, frigid conceits, and a self-conscious mix of the aestheticising and the violently melodramatic.

An example soon came up. Giulio Ricordi chose to stir up his potential composer–librettist team by getting them to revise the neglected *Simon Boccanegra*. Verdi acquiesced in language that was to be his throughout this last phase of his career: 'I am an *extra* [one who has outlived his normal career]; whatever I do will be an *extra*' (VR 80–81, 77).

The result, launched in 1881, did not persuade Verdi that *Boccanegra's* 'rickety table' had been made quite firm. A new scene did make a mark: a debate in the Genoa council chamber, followed by the bursting in of a mob, Simone's grand plea for peace, and a confrontation among all the chief characters. It was Verdi's own idea to have the Doge bring up an actual letter by Petrarch calling on Genoa and Venice to make peace in the name of the common Italian fatherland. Boito avoided Petrarch's name; he made the characters refer to 'the voice that thundered over Rienzi', 'the hermit of the Sorgue', and 'the singer of the blonde lady of Avignon' – sixth-form periphrases Verdi would never have put up with from his earlier librettists. In a coda of his own devising, Boito showed the villain forced to lay a curse on himself. Here Verdi's hankering after 'strong situations' made him fall in with the end-of-the-century cult of the elaborately lurid.

More preciosities marred the text of *Otello*, like Otello's parenthetical description of himself and his troops scaling enemy walls as 'ghastly ivy'. Boito himself was to write that his libretto 'illustrated' Shakespeare's tragedy.[7] There you have it, some modern Italian critics suggest: rather than recreate it as an Italian opera, like Piave with *Macbeth*, Boito nudged the audience into a European cultural operation.[8]

By the 1880s, however, Italian opera itself was no longer the swarming, uninhibited genre of Verdi's youth. Copyright, for one thing, made it a much bigger potential earner. New operas were now far fewer, but if successful they would bring in large rewards; publishers nursed them carefully and they took much longer to prepare. The near seven years that ran from Verdi's purchase of the *Otello* text to his finishing the score were unusual less in themselves than because as an 'extra' he could at any time choose to compose or not.

Some may relish the elaborate tiptoeing of Giulio Ricordi and Strepponi round the unpredictable composer, the veiled references to the 'chocolate project', the publisher's gifts of Christmas pastries decorated with a small Moorish figure, the resulting hints and jokes. Giulio steadily buttered up Verdi: his firm, he acknowledged at the start, had a material interest in a new Verdi opera, but he felt 'immense, unutterable emotion at the thought of a work that will make your name still more glorious, if such a thing is possible [...] in our frequent meetings Boito always spoke of Verdi with veneration and emotion; otherwise he would not be my friend' (VB, xxviii). He went on in the same vein. This did not prevent Verdi from now and then snapping at him and threatening to give up the whole thing.

Boito treated Verdi as a fellow-artist, with great courtesy and respect. Years after Verdi had started work, still without a fixed commitment, a newspaper reported Boito as having expressed regret at not setting *Otello* himself; Verdi offered to let him have it back. Boito, a musician neurotically dilatory but self-aware – he was to leave his own second opera unfinished after a half a century – begged Verdi to go on with the 'predestined' task: 'you are healthier than I, you are stronger than I [. . .] I shall know how to work for you, I who don't know how to work for myself, because you dwell in the true and real life of art, I in the world of delusions' (VB, 72–3). That momentary snag apart, all went smoothly between them thanks to Boito's full, persuasive letters, his welcome visits to Sant'Agata, the tact with which he offered to shorten some lines Verdi had not quite brought himself to declare too long; he became a friend.

Verdi composed *Otello* in bursts; for several months at a time he would let it lie fallow, or he would suggest that the project had gone cold on him. He also took time out in 1883 to revise and shorten *Don Carlos*, no light task; at most times he was busy running his estate and planning his cottage hospital. Only in 1885–86, when various European theatres were pressing him for the rights, did he begin to let on that *Otello* might be performed, and only on 1 November 1886 did he declare it finished. He then plunged into the business of producing it at La Scala, with himself, as he had insisted, in total control. The first night on 5 February 1887 – Faccio the conductor – was a triumph. Within the next two years or so productions in Rome, Vienna, London, and several Italian cities established it as the Verdi opera progressive music-lovers admired, even those who despised *Ernani* and *Rigoletto*. Verdi had renewed himself: at seventy-four he was the evergreen composer.

The opera was at first to have been called *Iago*, partly to avoid challenging Rossini's *Otello* – un-Shakespearian but admired – partly because the character fascinated Verdi: the old anticlerical liked to think of Iago as a smooth-talking priest. By 1886 he had come down firmly for *Otello*, a title the more suitable because the work is what Germans call 'literature opera': we cannot help asking how it squares up to Shakespeare's play.

Apt though modern criticisms of his diction are, Boito made an ingenious fist of cutting down and rearranging the tragedy; he dovetailed scenes and lines to give an already taut original a classic unity. Dropping the first, Venetian, act – some critics judge – blanks out Otello's stature and makes his brainwashing by Iago implausibly swift. This is to reckon without the power of music. Otello strides ashore; the storm subsides; the mere thirteen bars of his 'Esultate!' – Verdi's own idea – set him 'upon a peak of sublimity from which his descent will be all the more terrible'.[9] As an oasis amid Iago's machinations Boito, prompted by Verdi, devised the Act 2 serenade for Desdemona: this both affords a rest and gives a sense of time passing. The vividness of the Iago–Otello exchanges does whatever else is needed to stop hearers from worrying about plausibility.

What made the opera was the late style which Verdi had first deployed in the council chamber scene of the revised *Boccanegra*. There a string of musical lightning flashes makes for literally hair-raising drama. Both in voice and orchestra Verdi uses themes cut down to their essence, at times to fragments, yet they still work to bind the scene together; Simone's nobly expansive plea for peace leads to a powerful, highly articulated ensemble; the scene ends in more lightning flashes as the villain curses himself. It was a logical development of the technique first shown in Act 3 of *Rigoletto*.

In *Otello* too Verdi's 'microstructures' shape a 'many-faceted, prismatic discourse, constantly in high relief, as though etched by a radiant shaft of light'.[10] Nowhere does he write 'musical prose' or seek gradual transitions as in late Wagner. The opera works as a string of numbers – recitatives, choruses, arias, duets, a trio, a quartet, even a couple of strophic songs with ritornello (Iago's drinking song and Desdemona's haunting Willow Song) – all either miniaturised or, as they go on, transmuted.

'Esultate!' is the first of several musical epigrams stronger than most arias. Verdi builds the concerted pieces on the 'sectional' plan of the Violetta–Germont duet in *Traviata*, but with the sections now so slimmed down and the joins between them so cunning that we seem

23 Otello overhears Cassio and Iago joking about the handkerchief in the original Milan production, 1887. Contemporary engraving

to hear a freely developing exchange; in the Act 1 bonfire chorus musical ideas fly up so quick and spare that it seems over in a trice. Add orchestral writing of the utmost resource and delicacy – the muted fanfares during Otello's 'Ora e per sempre addio' have been compared to Mahler's, other passages to Brahms; the growled phrases with which the double basses herald Otello's entrance before the murder make a textbook example – and we are a long way from *Nabucco*.

Among the most memorable passages are the quietest: Iago's story of Cassio's dream, the trio in which he and Cassio laugh about the handkerchief while Otello eavesdrops, Otello's making up to Desdemona as to 'the cunning whore of Venice'. They achieve the sinister through rhythms or melodic patterns that suggest the courtly. 'Let us go back to the old: it will be a step forward?' But these are not the pastiche the mock eighteenth-century sections in Tchaikovsky's *The Queen of Spades* were to serve up three years later; as much as the lightning flashes in the revised *Boccanegra* they sound mint-new – Verdian 'inventions of the truth'.

The crown of the work is the love duet that ends the first act, itself the most satisfying of the four. Thanks to Boito as well as Verdi the duet does several things: it seals the peace after the tremendous, musically complex storm and the fight, it tells us about Otello's and Desdemona's courtship (brought in from Shakespeare's Venetian first act), it shows their very different personalities in happy balance, it voices the rapture the new-married pair serenely look forward to. Rarest of operatic emotions, intense, untroubled sexual love between husband and wife shapes from the beginning the solo cello line, the further consort of four cellos, and the heavenly coming together of winds, harp, and strings these lead on to, suggestive, as darker winds come in, of 'a deep but limpid pool'.[11] Though there are parallels, chiefly rhythmic, with the duet between those other newlyweds Elsa and Lohengrin – by the 1880s *Lohengrin* was a popular work in Italy – one might ask: is this not Verdi's challenge to what he admired about *Tristan und Isolde*, the duet at the heart of the 'night of love' in Act 2? Do not the rushing semiquavers as 'joy floods' Otello and Desdemona echo Tristan's approach after the dousing of the torch? It is as though Verdi had said 'I can do it all, and in less than a third of the time too.'[12]

Not all of Verdi's ideas work. Even in 1887 he thought an opera needed a big concerted finale with principals and chorus all lined up on stage. Boito skilfully got him off his first notion of an impending Turkish attack and onto the present Act 3 finale with its highly effective curtain (Otello strikes Desdemona before the ambassadors and, left alone with Iago – an episode moved from its earlier spot in the play – collapses in a fit). The finale was to carry forward the plot: 'time suspended' just before the act curtain no longer satisfied. Verdi worried at it, later revised it considerably for Paris, but could not make Iago's plan to murder Cassio reach the audience through the big ensemble noise – a token that although he could ram home a lightly disguised cabaletta (the oath-taking duet 'Sì, pel ciel marmoreo giuro' that closes Act 2), this kind of big concerted movement was now at odds with the rest of the opera as 'Ma tu, re' had not been with *Aida*.

It was Boito who thought up something at least as dubious – Iago's Credo. That Verdi at once hailed the text as 'Shakespearian through and through' (VB, 76) suggests a limited grasp of the play. Shakespeare's Iago baffles; Boito's spells out a late nineteenth-century diabolism. Though Verdi's incisive music carries all before it, the Credo remains a child of Boito's obsession with angel–devil, rose–worm duality.

Why does *Otello* with all its glories leave a touch of unease? We may in part blame Shakespeare: his tale of manipulation and handkerchiefs which a sensible word could at any moment undo runs awkwardly near farce. Boito's share in end-of-the-century decadence and – for Italian speakers – his overliterary language weigh on the opera. The Act 3 ensemble does not do all that Verdi wants. Yet opinions vary: after a close analysis of *Otello*'s structure and *tinta* Frits Noske can say that only with this work did Verdi raise Italian nineteenth-century opera 'to a level which, up to the present, appears unrivalled'.[13]

One handicap – the tenor who bellows and staggers through the title part – has been largely done away in our own time by the reign of Placido Domingo: Otello can awe without overpowering. As Verdi cast the original production he was troubled by the change that had come over the Italian singing profession. Many were now better at violent emotional outbursts than at clear timbre and accurate intonation; the few operas still current that required ornate singing had become vehicles for 'canary' sopranos. To Verdi, whose preferred Aida (along with Stolz) was the lucent, well-tuned Adelina Patti, this was dismaying.

Part of the problem was that he himself wanted singing actors rather than mere vocalists. From the 1857 *Boccanegra* the vocal line in his works no longer ran to coloratura, momentary special effects apart. For the villain in that opera he rejected one baritone as too short and myopic: whoever sang Paolo, a 'symbol of democracy' in a work about nobles and plebeians, should be not only an actor and good with words but handsome, imposing (BM, 395). In his way Verdi had joined the trend to greater realism. For the revised *Don Carlos* of 1884 he wished that in the final duet with Elisabeth the tenor 'would sing swooning, dreaming, with veiled voice etc., not propping himself up and staring at the conductor's beat'; the quartet should be '*acted*: not sung (badly at that) down by the footlights' (VR 82–85, 141).

The parenthesis 'badly at that' gave Verdi away: however much he wanted singers to act by the more realistic standards of the 1880s, they should sing well by the demanding technical standards of the 1840s. One exceptional singing actor did impose himself: Victor Maurel, who had satisfied Verdi as the 1881 *Boccanegra*, was the necessary Iago. Verdi, however, worried about the Otello: could the heroic tenor Francesco Tamagno sing in half voice such things as the love duet and the final 'dying upon a kiss'? Coached by Faccio and by Verdi himself, Tamagno overwhelmed early audiences – not, though, in half voice; what Shaw called his 'magnificent screaming'[14] fixed a tradition we are only now moving away from.

The worst problem was the Desdemona. Verdi at first made light of it. 'If [two candidates] sing ill, no matter! All the better, in fact – they will sing the more readily as I want them to'; yet he also made sure of their 'quality of voice and intonation and, of course, *intelligence* and *feeling* above all'. When Romilda Pantaleoni got the part he found her if anything 'too dramatic'; in early rehearsals her vocal problems alarmed him; even at her best she sang out of tune (VB, 94, 124; CV, IV, 86–7). He would clearly have dodged her or got rid of her if she had not been Faccio's mistress. As it was he kept quiet, saw her through, and, when at length she acknowledged that her voice was in trouble, counselled her frankly to give up later productions and rest. He cannot have missed the parallel with Strepponi in *Nabucco* forty-five years earlier, down to the behaviour of the Milan audience, who remembered the soprano's better days and treated her kindly.

Though in theoretical full control at Milan, Verdi later complained about the scenery and the out-of-tune double basses; he also objected to some of the artists in the next few productions elsewhere, which he did not supervise. The opera made its way regardless; yet Verdi got to the point of cursing it and wishing he had never written it.

This may have been passing bad temper. The 1880s, though not so tense for him as the 1870s, were punctuated by the death of friends, inevitable at the age he had reached but saddening. His great friend Clarina Maffei's partner Carlo Tenca died in 1883, her husband in 1885, Maffei herself – to Verdi's deep grief – in 1887; Opprandino Arrivabene had died in late 1886, Tito Ricordi was to die in 1888. Then Verdi's faithful amanuensis Muzio died in 1890, like his political friend Senator Piroli; Faccio, as good as dead in that year, died in 1891. All this fed an old man's pessimism. 'What have we achieved?' he asked Clarina Maffei after Tenca's death, 'What shall we achieve? . . . NOTHING!' – a pre-echo of Iago's 'death and then nothingness' (A, IV, 226–7).

In Italy these were years of severe economic and social troubles which the governments of Crispi and his immediate successors tried to master by imperial adventure and by force. Verdi had grown more conservative in his political outlook, and Strepponi in her religious outlook; extreme Catholic prejudice must have shaped the anti-semitic outburst with which she greeted news that Stolz's Jewish landlord wished to end her lease ('that Jew's proceeding is so ill-mannered and dishonest', she told Stolz, 'that I wished I could have walked with hobnailed boots on the heads of all Israel').[15] Verdi was to be in Milan from 7 to 9 May 1898 when the artillery fired into crowds of bread rioters, leaving eighty dead and 450 wounded; leaders of the Socialist parliamentary party were gaoled. According to Boito, who was there, Verdi 'witnessed the brawl [. . .] like an old mastiff calmly watching a lot of rabid poodles, he who remembers the generous struggles of 1848!' (VB, 491–2). Though Boito wrote out of his own prejudices, his account is plausible: Italian conservative liberals such as Verdi did fix a gulf between the limited political rights some had fought for in 1848 and workers' demand for a share in economic well-being. Verdi was to die in 1901 just as a more expansive, reforming period began under the prime minister Giovanni Giolitti.

Verdi and Strepponi may have lacked sympathy with whole classes of people – not to mention their own underlings as a group – but when individual hard cases came up they freely met them with charitable gifts. After Piave's incapacitating stroke in 1867 Verdi supported his wife, gave their daughter a 10,000-franc dowry, and promoted an album for the family's benefit; he later helped to maintain several old musicians or their widows, and by 1889 he had decided on the more ambitious scheme for a musicians' rest home that was to occupy his last years. He and his wife also gave money for the relief of flood or earthquake victims, the wounded of the Franco-Prussian war, and like causes. In his own neighbourhood Verdi's cottage hospital was his main charitable venture. Building or rebuilding tenants' houses he described in 1881 as charity: it gave people work and would not bring him in enhanced rents. It was, however, a capital investment; in 1881 economic pressures tended if anything to lower rents – as he was to accept some ten years later.

Even in the distressed 1880s and early 1890s, changes were coming over Italian society that heralded a move towards democracy. Industry was beginning to grow, elementary schools to cut into the illiterate mass, newspapers and illustrated journals to find more readers – chiefly in towns and chiefly in the north-west; already about 1880 Strepponi had named as grounds for no longer wintering in Genoa 'the coal smoke that, with the new commercial developments, now reaches us' (WalkerV, 442).

These changes explain the unprecedented demonstration that greeted Verdi at Turin railway station in 1894 when he caught a sleeper to Paris. Not students or musicians or operagoers but industrial workers, labourers, porters, military policemen, clerks left their posts, crowded round the train, and took their caps off; as the train began to move they cheered, men waving their caps, women their kerchiefs; Verdi, standing in the train door, waved back, visibly moved. Here was a consecration more meaningful than the Grand Officier grade of the Legion of Honour, given him after the Paris *Aida* in 1880, or the Grand Cross of the Italian order of St Maurice and St Lazarus, earned with *Otello* in 1887.

Most of those who crowded round Verdi's train had probably heard *Trovatore* or *Rigoletto* or *Aida* in one of the large popular-priced theatres that now gave such works; they had certainly heard bands play the Anvil Chorus, 'La donna è mobile', and the triumphal march. Few can have heard Verdi's latest opera, *Falstaff*, given in Milan the year before. It has never been truly popular, least of all in Italy. Though now fairly often done, it remains a connoisseur's piece.

'Have you ever thought of the enormous number of my years?' Verdi was nearly seventy-six when he asked Boito this question; when the completed work had its first performance he was nearly eighty. *Falstaff* ranks among the few dramatic masterpieces created in extreme old age; others are by Sophocles, Rameau, and Richard Strauss. Reasonably, Verdi was to ask from time to time whether he would enjoy life or strength enough to finish the opera. Yet in the same letter of July 1889 he remarked 'What joy to be able to tell the public: "We're still here! Roll up!"' (VB, 143).

It was Boito who suggested a comic opera based on *The Merry Wives of Windsor*, with Falstaff's persona built up through extracts from *Henry IV*. He pushed at an open door. Verdi had toyed with the possibility of a comic subject at least since 1868, as he emerged from *Don Carlos*'s vast gloom; then and later he had Falstaff in mind. Boito's sketch delighted him; but for the query about his age he plunged at once into detailed suggestions; within five weeks he wrote a comic fugue to end the work. In November Boito delivered the first two acts; by March 1890, when he sent in the last, Verdi had set the first. Full instrumentation, it is true, would as usual come later; now far too elaborate to be left to the rehearsal period, it was, Verdi felt, the heaviest part of his task.

Though Verdi spent almost endless pains on the composition of *Falstaff* – making minute changes up to the first night and beyond – his mood seems to have been calmer than in the days of *Otello*. Fallow intervals might still last as long as four months – breathing spaces rather than sulks, though melancholy at the death of friends played a part, as did a bout of illness and a troublesome lawsuit over French rights in earlier operas. Verdi called working on the score a pastime, but belied this with the intensity he brought to the task. As it neared the end he joked – in mock anger at Giulio Ricordi's having sent him an outsize Christmas pastry – 'It's true that as I get older I am growing quiet, patient, good-tempered, calm [. . .] [but] that won't keep me from the odd exceptional moment of obstinate fury, worse still than of old. Look out! Look out! Look out!!' (A, IV, 470).

The libretto needed few changes. Verdi asked for particular sounds and wordings; in the Windsor Forest scene he wanted Falstaff beaten, and he ended it with the comic fugue he had first thought of. He was to make further changes after the initial Milan run, but on musical–dramatic grounds, to tighten up moments that had gone slack in the theatre. Boito again did a remarkable job of slimming down the cast of characters, isolating crucial incidents, and dovetailing fragments of Shakespeare. It was his idea to give Anne and Fenton no full love duet but snatched exchanges, their intermittent larks and kisses punctuating the comedy 'as one sprinkles sugar over a pie' – one of the happiest things about the work (VB, 145, 150).

On the debit side, his language became yet more recondite than in *Otello*; he threw in archaic Italian words by the fistful, many in ensembles where different groups sing at the same time to different words and the audience catches virtually none. He meant to bring out the Italian origins of Shakespeare's comedy – which he and Verdi exaggerated from nationalistic motives: *Falstaff* was to disperse 'every kind of [musical] fog from beyond the Alps' (VB, 216). Audiences at the time failed to get the message, while to some later Italians Boito's diction made the work seem aestheticising, jewelled.

This would matter more if Verdi had not composed it with – his favourite prescription for singers – 'the devil in him'. Impish energy drives the first two acts in music both concise and fleet-footed; it surges back at the end after the lyrical pause of Fenton's sonnet and the enchantment of the Queen of the Fairies – her aria a full-length two stanzas, 'time suspended' for an ethereal moment.

The current runs strongest in the ensemble that brings Act 2 to a climax with the dumping of Falstaff into the Thames – one of the two passages Verdi tightened up after the first run. This time he discovered how to make a traditional finale, with the whole cast on stage, at once cohere musically and propel the drama. The wives round the laundry basket, Falstaff gasping for air, the lovers behind the screen, Ford and his band ready to pounce, make up a complex, rapidly shifting kaleidoscope, both musical precision engineering and irresistible farce. The other passage he revised – the women scatter after plotting the encounter at Herne's Oak, and Alice overhears Ford plan to betroth their daughter to Dr Caius – shows how a wisp of sound, a skipping theme once repeated, voices receding offstage, and a delicate orchestral coda for wind and strings can bridge farce and magic.

In *Otello* Verdi had miniaturised the forms of Italian romantic opera; in *Falstaff* he miniaturised himself. The women's and men's chattering ensembles rush by (all those inaudible words hewn from fourteenth-century classics); Falstaff's recall of his slenderness as a page makes an aria – thirty seconds long; Alice's 'Gaie comari di Windsor', about as short, eludes a cadence. Moments all hearers remember – Mistress Quickly's genuflecting phrase 'Reverenza', the tripping assignation 'Dalle due alle tre', the fatigued tramp-tramp of 'old John''s injunction to himself 'go thy ways', the mellifluous two-line motto the young lovers share – these crystallise a feeling, an attitude: it is as though an aria or a duet had been precipitated into a phrase. Orchestral comment, busy yet transparent, likewise catches a passing thought, like the hollow disaster that threatens 'if Falstaff should grow thin'. It is the 'flashes of lightning' method of the *Boccanegra* council chamber, though here – Ford's anguished monologue apart – the lightning bolts have turned into sparks, flickers, firefly signals cunningly organised.

Falstaff holds within itself the whole of Verdi's past practice, spun into an iridescent web. Strepponi talked of 'a new genre' (A, IV, 472); the genre contained one work, in its way near perfect. True, excess threatens as the fairies tickle and beat Falstaff; Mistress Quickly's otiose narrative – added because Giuseppina Pasqua delighted Verdi with her dramatic sense – overbears Alice's 'Gaie comari' immediately afterwards: minute flaws.

Falstaff's total gesture is uncanny. Though it has been called 'genial', its speed and its laughter show more than a touch of the ruthless, its mercurial darts a spiritual kinship with the Prestissimo con sordino movement in Bartók's fourth string quartet or the Allegro misterioso in Berg's Lyric Suite, not through likeness in compositional technique but because all three have an ear for the daemonic within. The final fugue is not genial but stringent. Verdi twice quoted its opening line ('All in the world's a joke') to Edoardo Mascheroni, the conductor of the early *Falstaff* performances, who had become a friend. To Boito he had quoted Falstaff's tirade against the world as 'thieving', 'shameless', 'wicked': 'I know it and, unfortunately, I've known it thirty years longer than you.' He meant it (C, 716, 718; VB, 176–7).

An opera finely calibrated in every bar, whose dialogue (ensembles apart) the audience must hear, needs a theatre smaller than most opera houses. Verdi, part way through composition, wanted such a theatre, but the economics of opera made him acquiesce in La Scala; later, in Paris, he was to choose the more intimate Opéra-Comique. The first night on 9 February 1893 was a great occasion rather than a solid hit. Verdi had again insisted on total control of casting and rehearsals: 'I won't complain', he told Ricordi, 'but if something is wanting I shall leave the theatre and you must then withdraw the score' (A, IV, 459). Grumblingly, he supervised the Rome and Paris stagings as well. In the year of the Paris *Falstaff*, 1894, the Opéra at length put on *Otello*, with Verdi's brilliant new ballet music: the eighty-one-year-old composer made the journey twice.

Maurel was the indispensable Falstaff both in Italy and in Paris, so indispensable that when, in Paris, he cut the big soliloquy – Falstaff broods on his ducking and feels the mulled wine warm him – Verdi's angry demand on Ricordi for an ultimatum got nowhere. The only other principal to satisfy Verdi completely was Pasqua. She became a friend and, like Stolz, was to share summer holidays at the Montecatini spa.

'It's all over!' That – Verdi later recalled – was his feeling after the third performance as he took leave of the Milan cast (A, IV, 497). They were to work together again in Rome and Paris, where his energy struck everybody, but with *Falstaff* his career in the theatre was at an end.

He still composed a little. In 1896–97 he wrote the Te Deum and Stabat Mater, first performed, with the earlier Laudi making up three 'sacred pieces', in Paris at Easter 1898; concert managers then put in as fourth the Ave Maria which Verdi had written as a pastime on an 'enigmatic scale'. The Te Deum, strongest of these, applies Verdi's refined late technique in the spirit of the Requiem.

Through the early 1890s Verdi's health seemed fair. Besides his usual sore throats and rheumatisms he had had occasional dizzy spells, one as far back as 1883 – perhaps minor strokes, but with no worse result than a feeling of weakness in the legs. This was a man who at sixty-one had had five teeth and a root taken out at one go. The person whose health roused concern was Strepponi. After years of stomach pains and arthritis she began in 1891 to feel nausea and loss of appetite – perhaps cancer symptoms; she ate little and in 1894 was described by a Paris interviewer as looking like an 'old bird' (IEV, 272). By 1897 she was weak and moved with difficulty; pneumonia carried her off on 14 November. In her will she looked forward to being reunited with 'my Verdi' in heaven. Whether he had been hers alone over the past twenty-five years we may doubt. But they had lived together for twice that, and had known each other for longer still; habit and sympathy told.

Verdi had himself suffered in January 1897 what was perhaps a minor stroke more serious than the earlier ones. Yet in 1898–99 he was a good deal recovered, enjoyed truffles and champagne, looked after

24 Verdi in the garden at Sant'Agata in extreme old age, with his sister-in-law Barberina Strepponi (seated, second from left), Teresa Stolz (standing, left), and Giulio Ricordi (standing, second from right) among others

the business of Sant'Agata, and had people to stay there – the usual ones, Stolz, Pasqua, Strepponi's sister Barberina (the sort of invalid who goes on forever), Giulio Ricordi and his wife, on occasion Boito. His daughter Maria and her family came and went. A harrowing episode – his seventeen-year-old grandson accidentally shot dead a housemaid – brought a verdict of manslaughter. The mild sentence perhaps deferred to Verdi's standing; the prompt royal pardon clearly did. We do not, however, know that Verdi acted in the matter but for thanking the king.

What chiefly took up these last years was the planning of Verdi's great project, the rest home for musicians. He had bought land for it in Milan in 1889; by 1894–95, with a neo-gothic design in hand by Boito's brother Camillo, he could get estimates and start building work. He took a keen interest in the details; at least once he climbed the scaffolding.

The project evolved in his mind from something like a hospice with uniformed inmates sleeping in dormitories, on the model of extant poorhouses, to a rest home with guests in everyday wear and individual double rooms; at an intermediate stage he thought of having them dress like him in old-fashioned clothes. The sums required were not small. In 1896 Verdi paid 400,000 francs (£16,000) towards building costs; in his will he endowed the home with 375,000 francs and his copyrights, and arranged for himself and Strepponi to be buried there. In December 1899 he signed the notarial act setting up the home; the necessary royal decree followed.

Verdi did all this just in time. Spiritually – we may guess – he was ready to go. 'My name is too old and boring!' he told Boito in December 1898; 'it bores me too'. By April 1900 he was writing 'I so badly need quiet!' (VB, 270; A, IV, 652). That summer the end seemed near. Yet in December he was able to go to his Milan hotel suite, as he now did for the winter. On 19 January 1901 a cerebral haemorrhage struck. As he lay in a coma Stolz and Maria looked after him; a priest called by Stolz gave extreme unction. On 27 January Verdi died. As his wife had been, he was temporarily laid in the town cemetery. On 26

February both were buried in the rest home; a large crowd attended; Toscanini conducted a choir 900 strong in 'Va, pensiero'.

By then the home was a going concern; it still is. So is nearly everything else that Verdi created. He built to last. In drama the only parallel is Shakespeare. Verdi is Shakespearean in his direct line to many levels of audience, his protean range, his inwardness with the human, and his ups and downs; above all in his stageworthiness over time. What the Victorian audience assumed and looked for we no longer share; yet nearly every one of Verdi's works can make good his call, at seventy-six: 'We're still here! Roll up!'

NOTES

Introduction: truth and theatre

1 I. Berlin, 'The naiveté of Verdi', in M. Chusid and W. Weaver, eds., *The Verdi Companion*, London, 1980, pp.1–12.
2 J.-G. Prod'homme, ed., 'Lettres inédites de Giuseppe Verdi à Léon Escudier', *Rivista musicale italiana* 35, 1928, pp. 519–52, esp. p. 534.
3 R. Parker, *Leonora's Last Act*, Princeton, 1997, pp. 105–6.

1 *The innkeeper's son, 1813–1842: Oberto to Nabucco*

1 Verdi's baptismal act and his entry in the civil register of births, both drawn up on 11 October, name the previous day as his date of birth. Verdi himself always celebrated his birthday on the 9th, which he said his mother had assured him was the right date. On such a matter, Luigia Verdi should have the benefit of the doubt.
2 The true birthplace, inhabited by the Verdis till 1830, was known as the 'old inn' or 'proprietor's house' (*casa padronale*), a term with no precise English equivalent ('manor house' would be too grand or too feudal); it suggests that the house was the most substantial building in the tiny settlement. See M. J. Phillips-Matz, *Verdi. A Biography*, Oxford, 1993, pp. 6–10.
3 Phillips-Matz, *Verdi*, p. 66.
4 This was in a letter to his librettist F. M. Piave, to whom he wrote in the slangy, bawdy terms common among theatre people (but otherwise uncommon in Verdi's correspondence). The word he applied to priests means literally 'testicle'.

5 Phillips-Matz, *Verdi*, p. 78.
6 Ibid., p. 102.
7 By the time Verdi gave his accounts of this episode, the old Italian system of opera seasons had broken down; he may have forgotten that Lent had once been regarded as a separate season. He may even have been unaware of it in 1841–42: Milan, a pioneer in such things, had opened up Lent for opera as early as 1788. That would explain his reported wrath at the failure to include *Nabucco* in the bill for the carnival season: it was normally billed as the 'carnival-Lent season', but Merelli, who was after all taking a chance on a work by a composer whose previous opera had been a total flop, may have chosen to present *Nabucco* as a separate, special Lenten opera.

2 *The galley slave, 1842–1847: Nabucco to Macbeth*

1 L. A. Garibaldi, ed., *Giuseppe Verdi nelle lettere di Emanuele Muzio ad Antonio Barezzi*, Milan, 1931, pp. 177–8.
2 Ibid., pp. 238, 244.
3 Ibid., p. 160.
4 E. Baker, ed., 'Lettere di Giuseppe Verdi a Francesco Maria Piave, 1843–1865', *Studi Verdiani* 4, 1986–87, pp. 136–66, esp. p. 157.
5 J. Budden, *The Operas of Verdi*, 3 vols., London, 1973–81, I, p. 212.
6 M. Pieri, *Viaggio da Verdi*, Parma, 1977, p. 30.
7 G. Baldini, *The Story of Giuseppe Verdi. Oberto to Un ballo in maschera*, Cambridge, 1980, pp. 70–1.
8 Baker, ed., 'Lettere a Piave', pp. 151, 152.
9 Baldini, *Story of Giuseppe Verdi*, p. 74.
10 G. B. Shaw, *Music in London 1890–1894*, 3 vols., London, 1932, II, p. 178.
11 Budden, *Operas of Verdi*, I, p. 152.
12 P. Gossett, 'The composition of "Ernani"', *Bollettino dell'Istituto di Studi Verdiani* 10, 1989, pp. 90–3.
13 Shaw, *Music in London*, II, p. 178.
14 Budden, *Operas of Verdi*, I, p. 275.
15 Prod'homme, ed., 'Lettres inédites à L. Escudier', p. 538.
16 F. Degrada, 'Lettura del *Macbeth*', in his *Il palazzo incantato*, 2 vols., Fiesole, 1979, II, pp. 79–137, esp. pp. 88, 101–2.

17 Budden, *Operas of Verdi*, I, p. 303.
18 Degrada, 'Lettura del *Macbeth*', II, p. 122.
19 Ibid., II, p. 115.

3 Turning-points, 1847–1849: I masnadieri to La battaglia di Legnano; Strepponi, revolution and Sant'Agata

1 Just when Verdi signed a contract with the Opéra management is unclear. The likelihood is that he discussed it informally on his brief visit to Paris at the beginning of June 1847, and reached a formal agreement on his return from London late in July.
2 Pieri, *Viaggio da Verdi*, pp. 105, 111.
3 E. Sala, 'Verdi e il teatro di boulevard parigino degli anni 1847–49', in P. Petrobelli and F. Della Seta, eds., *La realizzazione scenica dello spettacolo verdiano*, Parma, 1996, pp. 187–214. Verdi later told Piave that he did not know the play Piave referred to as *Stifelius*, but, as Sala points out, he may not have connected this with the original Paris title *Le Pasteur ou L'Évangile et le Foyer*.
4 Sala, ibid., suggests that the Rigoletto–Sparafucile dialogue in Act 2, spare and fragmentary over orchestral comment, derives from *mélodrame*. It may; there was, however, an operatic precedent in Donizetti's *Lucrezia Borgia* (1833).
5 For Cirelli's involvement with Strepponi: M. De Angelis, *Le carte dell'impresario*, Florence, 1982, pp. 155–9, 188.
6 Like most writers on Verdi I cannot accept Mary Jane Phillips-Matz's theory that the baby girl consigned to the Cremona orphanage in 1851 and registered as Santa Streppini, at a time when Strepponi and Verdi were living in seclusion not far away, was possibly or probably their child. To accept it one must suppose Strepponi and Verdi capable of thinking the change of one vowel would be disguise enough (or, if the change was the result of clerical error, of using Strepponi's own name in these particularly delicate circumstances). The rest of Phillips-Matz's evidence is circumstantial and could be readily explained in other ways. We should follow Occam's razor – the principle 'that for the purposes of explanation things not known to exist should not, unless it is absolutely necessary, be postulated as existing' (*Oxford English Dictionary*).

7 R. Parker, 'Arpa d'or dei fatidici vati'. The Verdian Patriotic Chorus in the 1840s, Parma, 1997.
8 A tacit subtext was that in the twelfth century Cremona had been the emperor Frederick Barbarossa's bastion against the rebel Lombard League of north Italian cities (the theme of Verdi's *La battaglia di Legnano* of 1849, which however shows another pro-imperial city, Como). The singers, Strepponi included, appeared for the celebratory hymn in medieval Cremonese costumes. To put it no higher, the emperor's visit was a reward for loyalty shown to his remote predecessor.
9 B. Pauls, *Giuseppe Verdi und das Risorgimento. Ein politischer Mythos im Prozess der Nationenbildung*, Berlin, 1996 (see my review in Studi Verdiani 12, 1997, pp. 203–8).
10 Phillips-Matz, *Verdi*, pp. 251–2.
11 G. P. Minardi, ed., 'Appunti inediti di Bruno Barilli su Verdi', Bollettino dell'Istituto di Studi Verdiani 1, 1960, pp. 220–8, esp. p. 227.
12 Phillips-Matz, *Verdi*, p. 288. This author's belief that Verdi in 1850–51 was going through a profound crisis rests on her assumption that the child Santa Streppini, born about this time, was probably Strepponi's (and perhaps his) and that this poisoned relations with Carlo and Luigia Verdi. If, as I argue, we have no grounds for entertaining the assumption the quarrel with his parents can be seen as an episode, sour while it lasted but neither untypical nor necessarily traumatic.

4 *The people's composer, 1849–1859: Luisa Miller to Un ballo in maschera*

1 Literalists may object that the interior of Africa had not yet been 'opened up'. There were, however, European or Europeanised groups in Egypt, Algeria, the Cape, the Boer republics, and the Spanish and Portuguese territories. A military band in any of these places was almost bound to play Verdi's music, as British bands did in India.
2 See G. Schmidgall, 'Verdi's *King Lear* project', Nineteenth-Century Music 9, 1985, pp. 83–101; also the penetrating criticism of Baldini, *Story of Giuseppe Verdi*, pp. 122, 179, 187–9.

3 Baker, ed., 'Lettere a Piave', p. 159.
4 P. Gossett, 'New sources for Stiffelio: a preliminary report', in M. Chusid, ed., *Verdi's Middle Period 1849–1859*, Chicago, 1997, pp. 19–43, esp. pp. 42–3.
5 Budden, *Operas of Verdi*, I, pp. 500–1.
6 C. M. Mossa, 'La genesi del libretto del "Trovatore"', *Studi Verdiani* 8, 1992, pp. 52–103, esp. p. 71.
7 C. Dahlhaus, *Realism in Nineteenth-Century Music*, Cambridge, 1985, p. 64.
8 Shaw, *Music in London*, I, p. 178.
9 P. Pinagli, *Romanticismo di Verdi*, Florence, 1967, p. 27.
10 Dahlhaus, *Realism in Nineteenth-Century Music*, pp. 66–8.
11 See also F. Walker, ed., 'Unpublished letters', *Bollettino dell'Istituto di Studi Verdiani* 1, 1960, pp. 28–43 (esp. p. 33).
12 Pauls, *Giuseppe Verdi und das Risorgimento*, pp. 223–47, argues that the proposed new libretto was not so very unlike Somma's and was therefore acceptable, that Verdi's objections were a put-up job, and that he deliberately provoked a breach, essentially to serve Ricordi's interests over possible piracy of the score in Naples. Verdi, she concludes, is supposed to have dug in his heels because he wanted to preserve the element of tyrannicide in the plot, but he was really interested in preserving his and Ricordi's copyright; Puritan Boston as the locale he accepted for the Rome version was a big change, about as incongruous as medieval Florence would have been; his insistence on a brilliant court was a mere pretext. All this seems ill judged:

(a) Verdi's whole relationship with Ricordi shows him to have been far from a catspaw; he minded about his copyright, but nowhere else in his career is there any sign of his putting it ahead of getting a first performance right. That Ricordi was anxious about the Naples situation is not evidence of Verdi's motives.

(b) It is extremely doubtful that Verdi set much store by the theme of tyrannicide in *Ballo*, as alleged by the 'Risorgimento' interpretation Pauls wishes to refute (an interpretation, for this opera, not widely shared). But for perfunctory talk in the libretto of Riccardo's tyrannical acts as the personal motive driving the conspirators (imposed by the censor to avoid any idea of a political cause) he is shown as a highly sympathetic character. Pauls's further argument that Naples in December 1858 approved *Ballo* in its Rome version, and therefore did not much mind tyrannicide, leaves out of account (i) the difference at institutional level between a ruler and a governor (ii) the difference, important in Italy at that date, between sponsoring the first performance of a work and putting it on after it had been launched elsewhere: the owners of La Fenice put on *I due Foscari* after its first production in Rome, though they had earlier declined to originate it for fear of upsetting fellow Venetian noble families.

(c) Talk of Puritan Boston assumes knowledge Italian audiences lacked: to them (natives of a country that had long since lost any ocean-going merchant fleet) early colonial America was a virtual closed book; no trace of Puritanism appears in the libretto, which might as well have been set in royalist Baltimore. (Why was it not? Because if Italians knew little of Boston – save that, happily for the censor, it was far away – they knew nothing of Baltimore.) Altogether it is hard to see why we should dismiss Verdi's repeated, forceful, and (if we listen) cogent argument that his music depended on the opera's being set in a brilliant court. True, he does seem to have been trailing his coat: he had a legitimate grievance against Naples for its travesty of *Rigoletto* and *Traviata*, and his standing was such that he could put on *Ballo* in an acceptable version almost anywhere else in Italy. He was, however, willing to fulfil his Naples contract by staging it there in a version very like that later agreed for Rome (it would have been set in an equally semi-mythical seventeenth-century court of Pomerania). The setting of *Ballo* matters little provided that, as Verdi asked, it combines a brilliant court life and belief in witchcraft: the seventeenth century does better than 'historic' 1792. Scribe's concoction anyhow has little to do with history.

13 H. S. Powers, '"La dama velata": Act II of *Un ballo in maschera*', in Chusid, ed., *Verdi's Middle Period*, pp. 273–336 (esp. pp. 293–4).
14 Ibid., pp. 289–92.
15 Ibid., p. 329.

5 Complications, 1859–1872: La forza del destino, Don Carlos and Aida

1 G. Martin, ed., 'Unpublished letters. A contribution to the history of *La forza del destino*', *Bollettino dell'Istituto di Studi Verdiani* 3, 1962, pp. 745–54, esp. p. 751.
2 Degrada, 'Lettura del *Macbeth*', p. 127.
3 To Faccio, [Jan. 1879], in R. De Rensis, *Franco Faccio e Verdi*, Milan, 1934, pp. 182–5.
4 G. Azzaroni and P. Bignami, *Corticelli Mauro impresario*, Bologna, 1990, pp. 166–9. Verdi as landowner is usefully documented in F. Cafasi, *Giuseppe Verdi fattore di Sant'Agata*, Parma-Busseto, 1994, on which much of the following section is based. Unpublished evidence, however, may well exist which an economic historian could use to make a systematic study. All we now have are anecdotal evidence and fragmentary data: any conclusions must be tentative.
5 See also Walker, 'Unpublished letters', p. 37.
6 The following pages are based largely on WalkerV, 283–446, a detailed and perceptive account of the Verdi–Mariani–Stolz affair that seems unlikely to be superseded. References are given only to other sources.
7 This sentence is deleted in Strepponi's letter book, but in the draft she did send she said much the same thing at greater length.
8 Strepponi's draft, which begins as a diary entry and turns into a letter, is full of alterations, deletions, and alternative passages. WalkerV, 431–2, gives most of these, but they are here left out.
9 Phillips-Matz, *Verdi*, p. 756.
10 F. Noske, *The Signifier and the Signified*, Oxford, 1990, p. 202.
11 Budden, *Operas of Verdi*, III, p. 157.
12 Ibid., III, p. 120.
13 Parker, *Leonora's Last Act*, p. 18.
14 Strictly speaking, Gladstone invested in Turkish bonds secured on the tribute which the loosely dependent Egyptian government paid to Constantinople. Verdi's investments other than in land or Italian government bonds are not known; they were generally made in Paris.

15 Budden, *Operas of Verdi*, III, p. 251.
16 Ibid., III, p. 231.

6 Evergreen, 1872–1901: the Requiem, Otello, and Falstaff

1 G. B. Shaw, 'A word more about Verdi', in his *London Music in 1888–89 as heard by Corno di Bassetto*, London, 1937, p. 387.
2 Shaw, *Music in London*, I, p. 247.
3 To Alberto Mazzucato, 20 March 1868, *Atti del II.o congresso internazionale di studi verdiani, Verona 1969*, Parma, 1971, pp. 540–1. See also G. W. Harwood, 'Verdi's reform of the Italian opera orchestra', *19th Century Music* 10, 1986–7, pp. 108–34.
4 Petrobelli and Della Seta, eds., *La realizzazione scenica dello spettacolo verdiano*, pp. 270, 272, and passim.
5 Pieri, *Viaggio da Verdi*, p. 114.
6 De Rensis, *Faccio e Verdi*, p. 128.
7 To Verdi, 10 May 1886, VB, 104. Boito contrasted his own work – which he saw as 'illustrating' or 'interpreting the spirit' of the play – with a translation, which had to be as faithful as possible to the letter of the original. His use of the verb 'to illustrate' is none the less revealing.
8 Such critics include Baldini, Pieri, and Degrada, already referred to, D. Goldin, *La vera fenice*, Turin, 1985, and – particularly scathing – G. Morelli, 'Qualcosa sul Nerone', in *Arrigo Boito*, Florence, 1994, pp. 519–55. See also Noske, 'Otello: drama through structure', in his *The Signifier and the Signified*, pp. 133–70, and J. Kerman, *Opera as Drama*, New York, 1956, both more critical of Boito than English-speaking writers were in the first half of the twentieth century; and, more favourable to Boito, especially to his command of metre and sound patterns, E. Sala Di Felice, 'Ricodificazione come interpretazione. "Otello" tra Boito e Verdi', *Studi Verdiani* 12, 1997, pp. 11–30.
9 Budden, *Operas of Verdi*, III, p. 338.
10 Pieri, *Viaggio da Verdi*, p. 162.
11 Budden, *Operas of Verdi*, III, p. 352.
12 Verdi's remarks about *Tristan und Isolde* come in a very late interview in the winter of 1898–99 (IEV, 329). He owned a score, however, and

could well have read it by the 1880s. See L. Magnani, 'L'"ignoranza musicale" di Verdi e la biblioteca di Sant'Agata', *Atti del III.o congresso internazionale di studi verdiani: Milano 1972, Parma, 1974*, pp. 250–7.
13 Noske, *The Signifier and the Signified*, p. 170.
14 Shaw, *London Music in 1888–89*, p. 171.
15 A, IV, 128–9. There is no evidence of anti-Semitic feeling in Strepponi's earlier letters. She, Verdi, and many other members of the opera world on occasion applied 'Jew' or 'Jewish' to a gentile as an equivalent of 'miser' or 'mean', but that primitive usage, common in the early nineteenth century, did not denote modern, systematic anti-Semitism, which in Italy as elsewhere in Europe grew late in the century.

FURTHER READING

No life of Verdi so far is both complete and satisfactory. The best book on him is still Frank Walker, *The Man Verdi*, London, 1962; but rather than a full biography it is an acute, carefully documented study of important aspects of Verdi's life, in particular his relationship with his home town, with Giuseppina Strepponi, and with Angelo Mariani and Teresa Stolz.

M. J. Phillips-Matz, *Verdi. A Biography*, Oxford, 1993, chronicles in detail one happening after another throughout Verdi's life; it is strong on people, places, and accurate records of his youth, but it does not consider the music, is uncritical about Verdi as landowner, and recycles myths about his share in Italian nationalism. This last is true also of G. Martin, *Verdi*, New York, 1963, and C. Osborne, *Verdi: a Life in the Theatre*, London, 1987, built around generous quotations from Verdi's letters, some of which Osborne had previously translated in *The Letters of Giuseppe Verdi*, London, 1971. G. Baldini, *The Story of Giuseppe Verdi*, Cambridge, 1980, in contrast is an innovatory study of both the life and the music. Unfortunately the author died part way through: the book stops at 1859 and *Un ballo in maschera*. The earlier life by F. Toye (1931) is out of date, as is that by C. Gatti (2nd edn 1951, Eng. transl. 1955).

Of the many Italian lives since Gatti's original edition of 1931, the great disappointment is F. Abbiati, *Giuseppe Verdi*, 4 vols., Milan, 1959. This was to have been a complete, near-definitive life; the author saw many new documents, but he misunderstood or mistranscribed some of them, and spoilt his work with invented conversations and self-indulgent commentary. It is still an important source – to be used with care.

There should one day be a complete edition of Verdi's letters, run by the Istituto Nazionale di Studi Verdiani at Parma. The editing of the first volumes is exemplary; they print correspondence with Ricordi in 1880–81 and 1882–85 and with Boito (see list of abbreviations). The institute also holds on microfilm all of Verdi's (and his disciple Muzio's) letters to Ricordi. Meanwhile the most important printed source remains I copialettere di Giuseppe Verdi, ed. G. Cesari and A. Luzio, Milan, 1913, reprinted Sala Bolognese, 1987 – minutes from Verdi's letter-books, not always identical with the letters as sent; it also prints extracts from his correspondence with Clarina Maffei and others. Carteggi Verdiani, ed. A. Luzio, 4 vols., Rome, 1935, 1947, includes letters of others besides Verdi. It is not always reliable: by the 1930s Luzio, a renowned archivist, was willing tacitly to suppress awkward material. Giuseppe Verdi nelle lettere di Emanuele Muzio ad Antonio Barezzi, ed. L. A. Garibaldi, Milan, 1931, gives a lively account of Verdi in his thirties; some of Verdi's unbuttoned letters to F. M. Piave are published by Evan Baker in Studi Verdiani 4, 1986–87, pp. 136–66. Verdi intimo, ed. A. Alberti, Milan, 1931, prints Verdi's letters to Opprandino Arrivabene in the latter part of his life.

Three books edited by H. Busch collect evidence of the making of one or more operas: Aida, Minneapolis, 1978, Otello and the revised Simon Boccanegra, Oxford, 1988, and Falstaff, Bloomington, 1997. M. Conati, La bottega della musica, Milan, 1983, covers the making of the five operas Verdi wrote for Venice; D. Rosen and A. Porter, eds., Verdi's 'Macbeth': a Sourcebook, Cambridge, 1984, studies both the making of an opera and its after-life.

Studies of the music have proliferated in the past forty years or so. They are dominated by Julian Budden's The Operas of Verdi, 3 vols., London, 1973–81, revised edn 3 vols., Oxford, 1992; besides a detailed analysis of individual works, each volume has an enlightening chapter on the state of Italian opera during Verdi's early, middle, and late phases. Budden has also written the volume on *Verdi* in the Master Musicians series, London, 1985. P. Petrobelli, *Music in the Theater*, Princeton, 1994, includes several fundamental studies of Verdi's composing process. J. Hepokoski has published in the Cambridge Opera Handbooks series outstanding studies of *Otello* (1987) and *Falstaff* (1983); there are also a study of the Requiem by D. Rosen (Cambridge, 1995), and shorter volumes on a number of operas in the English National Opera Handbooks series, all edited by N. John.

Only one of Verdi's librettists is the subject of a book in English: J. N. Black, *The Italian Romantic Libretto: a study of Salvadore Cammarano* (Edinburgh, 1984). Two books of mine study Italian opera management: *The Opera Industry in Italy from Cimarosa to Verdi. The Role of the Impresario*, Cambridge, 1984, and – less detailed – *Music and Musicians in Nineteenth-Century Italy*, London, 1991.

Readers wanting fuller bibliographies should go to the essays on Verdi by Andrew Porter in *The New Grove Dictionary of Music and Musicians*, London, 1980 (a new edition of which is due shortly), and by Roger Parker in *The New Grove Dictionary of Opera*, London, 1992, themselves well worth reading; Porter's is reprinted in *The New Grove Masters of Italian Opera*, London, 1983, edited, like the dictionaries, by S. Sadie. Each volume of the periodical *Studi Verdiani* gives a fuller year-by-year bibliography.

INDEX

Note: to avoid replication, the index has no entry for Giuseppe Verdi. His relationships and aspects of his life and career are dealt with under individual and subject entries. Each of his operas has an entry; works by others are entered under their composers or authors.

Abbiati, Franco, 197–8
Aida, 2, 3, 7, 65, 83, 118, 122, 139–43, passim, 146, 148–54, 158–9, 164, 176
Alzira, 36, 37, 47
Argentina, 88, 155
Aroldo, 91, 113, 114, 134
Arrivabene, Count Opprandino, 38, 178
Auber, Daniel
  Gustave III, 116
Austria
  as Italian power, 20–1, 73
  Church policy, 91
Attila, 2, 3, 36, 37, 43, 45–6, 50, 53, 54
  'nationalistic', 76–7
Avanzi, Canon Giovanni, 161, 165

Bach, Johann Sebastian, 166
Baldini, Gabriele, 92, 103, 105
Ballo in maschera, Un, 7, 8, 34, 114–19, 135, 192–3
Barezzi, Antonio, 10, 15–20, 23–5, 29, 80–2, 133
Barezzi, Giovanni, 134

Barezzi (later Verdi), Margherita, 4, 18, 24, 25–7, 30
Battaglia di Legnano, La, 8, 61, 79–80, 88, 89
Baudelaire, Charles, 57
Beethoven, Ludwig van, 166
Bellini, Vincenzo, 21, 29, 35, 36, 41, 44, 48, 50, 61, 95
  Norma, 41, 44, 66, 75, 76, 100, 112
  Puritani, I, 52
Berlin, Sir Isaiah, 1, 4
Berlioz, Hector, 1, 35, 113, 166
Birth and childhood, 4, 12–17
Bizet, Georges
  Carmen, 109, 156
Boito, Arrigo, 126–7, 165, 169–76, 178–9, 180–1, 186
  Mefistofele, 170
Boito, Camillo, 186
Busseto, 9–19, passim, 23–7, 70
  Verdi's and Strepponi's resentment of, 25, 80–2, 132–4
Byron, George Gordon, Lord, 21

Cammarano, Salvadore, 47, 89, 92, 101–3

Carlyle, Thomas
    Past and Present, 42–3
Carrara, Angiolo, 130, 133
Cather, Willa
    The Song of the Lark, 6
Cavour, Count Camillo, 122–3, 131
Censorship, 75–7, 90–4, 101–2, 116–17
Charity, 128, 179, 186–7
Church music, 17, 18
    Requiem, 143, 160–3, 169
    Sacred Pieces, 163, 184
Cirelli, Camillo, 68–9
Corsaro, Il, 53–4, 80
Corticelli, Mauro, 128, 134, 139

Dahlhaus, Carl, 105, 111
Degrada, Francesco, 56, 57
Delacroix, Eugène, 45
Demaldè, Giuseppe, 10, 24, 75
Dérivis, Prosper, 33
De Sanctis, Caterina, 71–2
Dickens, Charles, 2–3
Domingo, Placido, 176
Don Carlos, 7, 136, 146–8, 151, 160, 169, 172, 177
Donizetti, Gaetano, 4, 21, 29, 35, 36, 48, 50, 54, 61, 95, 127
    Le Duc d'Albe, 4
    Torquato Tasso, 44
Due Foscari, I, 41, 44, 193
Du Locle, Camille, 148–9
Dumas fils, Alexandre
    La Dame aux camélias, 102, 107

Education, 12–22
Egypt, 149–50
Elder, Mark, 114
Ernani, 7, 37, 41, 47–50, 52, 79, 83, 105
    censorship, 76, 77
Escudier, Léon, 89

Faccio, Franco, 126–7, 165, 169, 170, 172, 177, 178
Falstaff, 5, 7, 36, 164, 180–4

Family origins, 12–14
Fauré, Gabriel
    Requiem, 163
Ferrari, Giovanni, 24, 25
Florence
    Teatro della Pergola, 54, 160
Forza del destino, La, 8, 124–6, 159, 163
France
    Legion of Honour, 72, 180
    political and cultural influence, 21, 114–17, 122, 167
    1848 revolution, 72, 78
Frezzolini, Erminia, 52

Galletti, Isabella, 139, 140
Garibaldi, Giuseppe, 123, 161
Gatti, Carlo, 7
Genoa, 83, 134–41, passim, 146, 179
Ghislanzoni, Antonio, 150–1
Gilbert and Sullivan, 49
Gioberti, Vincenzo
    Of the Civil and Moral Primacy of the Italians, 42–3, 72–5, passim, 79
Giorno di regno, Un, 30–1
Giovanna d'Arco, 31, 36, 41, 43–4, 45, 77
Gladstone, William Ewart, 5–6, 149
Gossett, Philip, 98
Guasco, Carlo, 52
Gutiérrez, García, 102, 114

Haydn, Joseph
    The Creation, 22–3
Hugo, Victor, 3, 56, 65
    Hernani, 47
    Roi s'amuse, Le, 40–1, 91, 92

Illness and death, 36–7, 101, 184–7
Italy
    clericalism and anticlericalism, 9–10, 17, 19, 23–5, 129–30, 161
    language and dialects, 15
    musical tradition, 22, 126–7, 165–7, 181
    nationalism, 73–80, 107

Italy (cont.)
  patronage and official recognition, 164–5, 180, 186
  post-unity politics and disturbances, 123, 131, 149–50, 178–80
  revolutions and wars, 9–10, 72–80, 107, 119, 122

Jacovacci, Vincenzo, 117
Jérusalem, 61, 63, 72, 83
Joyce, James
  Portrait of the Artist as a Young Man, 163

Lamennais, Félicité-Robert de
  A Believer Speaks, 42–3
Lanari, Alessandro, 54, 66, 113
Lavigna, Vincenzo, 20, 22
Lind, Jenny, 61
Loewe, Sofia, 47, 52
Lombardi alla prima crociata, I, 36, 41, 43, 45, 52, 66
  'nationalistic', 74, 75, 76
London, 53, 61–2, 124
  Covent Garden, 2, 3, 159
  Sadler's Wells, 2
  St Pancras Town Hall, 48
Lord Hamilton, 28
Louis-Phillippe, King, 72
Lucca, Francesco and Giovannina, 53–4, 140, 155–6
Luisa Miller, 4, 8, 31, 63, 89
Lumley, Benjamin, 61

Macbeth, 7, 35, 37, 41, 50, 51, 53, 54–9, 65, 83, 89, 95–6, 98, 171
Maffei, Andrea, 38, 47, 61, 178
Maffei, Clara (Clarina), Countess, 34, 38, 79, 143, 161, 165, 178
Manton, Franz, 48
Manzocchi, Almerinda, 51
Manzoni, Alessandro, 160–1
  The Betrothed, 3, 21, 161
Mariani, Angelo, 134–41, 169

Marie-Louise, ex-empress, Duchess of Parma, 10, 66, 75
Mariette, Auguste, 149
Marzi, Ercole and Luciano, 113
Mascheroni, Edoardo, 183
Masnadieri, I, 53, 61, 83
Massini, Pietro, 23, 28
Maurel, Victor, 177, 183–4
Mazzini, Giuseppe, 75, 78, 79, 123
Mélodrame, 65, 100, 109, 190
Mendelssohn, Felix, 166
Mercadante, Saverio, 29, 42
Merelli, Bartolomeo, 28–33, passim, 45, 54, 113, 125
Meyerbeer, Giacomo, 64, 112, 126, 127, 134, 156
  Africaine, L', 112, 124
  Huguenots, Les, 159
  Prophète, Le, 112
  Robert le Diable, 57–63
Milan
  Conservatorio, 18–20
  as intellectual and operatic capital, 20–1, 22, 189
  1898 disturbances, 178–9
  Teatro alla Scala, 20, 21, 27–8, 45, 54, 77, 125, 156, 159, 183
Miller, Jonathan, 103
Monza, 24, 25
Moriani, Napoleone, 29
Moshinsky, Elijah, 43
Mozart, Wolfgang Amadeus, 166
  Don Giovanni, 118
Musorgsky, Modest
  Boris Godunov, 125
Muzio, Emanuele, 25, 36, 37, 38, 61, 133, 135, 140, 178

Nabucco, 30–3, 34, 37, 41, 43, 44–5, 52, 53, 65, 66
  'nationalistic', 73–5, 76
Naples
  Teatro San Carlo, 79, 89, 116–17, 159, 192–3
Napoleon, emperor, 9, 12

Napoleon III, emperor, 80, 112, 116, 122, 146
Nicolai, Otto, 51
Noske, Frits, 176

Oberto, conte di San Bonifacio, 27–9, 31
Opera
  compositional methods, 34–7
  contracts, copyright, and business dealings, 4–5, 36, 61, 87–90
  earnings, 35, 54, 61, 86–90, 124, 146
  structure, style, and technique, 3–4, 41–5, 57–8, 94–101, 114–16, 150–2, 159–60, 181–3
  system production, 27, 34–6, 126, 155–6, 159–60
  vocal casting, 50–2, 176–7
  worldwide diffusion, 86–7
Otello, 5, 7, 88, 164, 169–78, 181, 182, 183

Pacini, Giovanni, 35, 124
Pallavicino, Marchesa Luisa Sauli-, 136, 141
Pantaleoni, Romilda, 177–8
Paris, 64–5
  Opéra, 35, 61–5, 112–13, 124, 146–7, 155, 159
  Opéra-Comique, 183
Parker, Roger, 74
Parma, city and duchy, 9–10, 12, 18, 24–5, 122–3, 159, 165
Pasqua, Giuseppina, 183, 184, 186
Patti, Adelina, 51–2, 176
Petrobelli, Pierluigi, 95–6, 105, 152
Phillips-Matz, Mary Jane, 12, 190, 191, 197
Piave, Francesco Maria, 34, 76, 92–5, passim, 108, 124, 150, 171
  as friend and chief librettist, 38, 39–41, 46–8, 56, 179
Piazza, Antonio, 28, 29
Piroli, Giuseppe, 131, 178

Pius IX, Pope, 72, 150
Powers, Harold S., 118, 119
Provesi, Ferdinando, 10, 18, 23
Publicity, 6, 156–8, 164
Publishers, 52–4, 155–8
Puccini, Giacomo, 110, 163
  La bohème, 86
Religious and moral outlook, 30, 161–3
Reputation, 2–3, 123–4, 158–9
Ricordi, publisher, 4–5, 61, 88–90, 91, 127, 140, 155–8, 164, 169, 192
  family, 134, 186
  Giovanni, 53, 157
  Giulio, 155–8, 169–71, 181, 184
  Tito, 135, 156–7, 159
Rigoletto, 2, 7, 8, 31, 40–1, 65, 83, 86, 91–101, 103, 173
  censorship, 91–4, 116
Risorgimento, *see* Italy, nationalism
Rochester, 28
Romanticism, 42–3, 94
Roncole, 12, 14, 15
Ronconi, Giorgio, 29, 33, 44
Rossini, Gioachino, 19, 21, 22, 23, 29, 30, 36, 50, 61, 157–8
  and operatic forms, 42, 95
  Barber of Seville, The, 36, 147
  Maometto II, 41
  Mosè in Egitto, 33, 41
  Otello, 172
  political outlook, 74
  Requiem Mass for, 138–9, 160
  Semiramide, 41, 42, 98
  Verdi's view of, 95, 147, 166
  William Tell, 147

Said, Edward, 149
St Petersburg, 124
Salvini-Donatelli, Fanny, 108
Sant' Agata, 12, 78, 82–5, 90, 128–33, 161
Scapigliati ('dishevelled ones'), 126
Schiller, Friedrich, 21, 43, 56, 146
Schlegel, August Wilhelm, 57

Scribe, Eugène, 4, 112–13, 116, 118
Sexuality and marriage, 6, 22, 39–41, 70
  see also Barezzi, Margherita; Stolz, Teresa; Strepponi, Giuseppina
Shakespeare, William, 54–6, 187
  Hamlet, 56
  Henry IV, 180
  King Lear, 56, 91–2, 99, 106, 116
  Macbeth, 54–9, 124
  Merry Wives of Windsor, The, 180
  Othello, 54, 56, 169–76, passim
Shaw, George Bernard, 48, 50, 106, 109, 158, 177
Shelley, Percy Bysshe
  Prometheus Unbound, 73
Simon Boccanegra, 8, 31, 113–14, 125, 170–1, 173, 177
Social life, 37–8
Solera, Temistocle, 29, 31, 43, 45–6, 48, 76–7
Somma, Antonio, 92, 116
Sonzogno, Edoardo, 156
Spezia, Maria, 108
Staël, Mme de
  On Germany, 43
Stiffelio, 2, 65, 90–1, 98, 113
Stolz, Teresa, 6, 134, 136–46, 176, 184, 186
Strepponi, Barberina, 186
Strepponi (later Verdi), Giuseppina, ix, 6, 29, 33, 63, 124, 158, 171, 177–8
  and Mariani, 134–41, passim
  and Sant' Agata, 83–5, 132
  children (Camillo, Sinforosa, Adelina), 66, 68–9, 70, 80, 190, 191
  death and burial, 184, 186–7
  early relationship with Verdi, 39, 65–72, 80–2
  later married life, 121–2, 136–46
  marriage, 70
  religion, 71, 161, 178

String quartet in E minor, 127
Sutherland, Joan, 51

Tadolini, Eugenia, 51, 68
Tamagno, Francesco, 177
Tchaikovsky, Piotr Ilych
  The Queen of Spades, 175
Tenca, Carlo, 178
Tinsley, Pauline, 48
Toscanini, Arturo, 159–60, 187
Traviata, La, 2, 7, 31, 47, 49, 69, 86, 101, 107–12, 173
Trovatore, Il, 2, 7, 47, 86, 89, 90, 95, 101–7, 113, 114, 125
Truthfulness, in Verdi's life and work, 1, 4–7, 25, 30, 87
Turin, 123, 179–80

Varesi, Felice, 44, 56, 94, 108
Vaughan Williams, Ralph, 101
Vêpres siciliennes, Les, 4, 112–13, 146
Venice, 37, 77, 122, 146
  Teatro La Fenice, 77, 92–4, passim, 107–8, 160, 193
  Teatro San Benedetto
Verdi, Carlo, 10, 14, 15–16, 80, 83–5, 133
Verdi, (Filomena) Maria, 71, 133, 186
Verdi, Giuseppa, 12
Verdi, Luigia (née Uttini), 9, 10, 15–16, 83–5
Verdi, Virginia and Icilio Romano, 4, 26–7, 30
Victor Emmanuel II, King, 74

Wagner, Richard, 1, 3, 7, 56, 95, 126, 156, 158–9, 173
  Lohengrin, 140, 175
  Tristan und Isolde, 119, 175
  Verdi's view of, 166–7
Walker, Frank, ix, 39–71, 135, 197
Webster, John, 103
Werner, Zacharias
  Attile, König der Hunnen, 43, 76